PRACTICAL COUNSEL
AND
Heavenly Wisdom

May the Lord God Almighty bless those who read this book with His love, joy, and peace.

With love,
Georgia
Gorham-Brockman

Practical Counsel and Heavenly Wisdom

Helpful Advice for the Christian Walk

Georgia Gorham-Brockman

© 2015 by Georgia Gorham-Brockman. All rights reserved.

Published by Redemption Press, PO Box 427, Enumclaw, WA 98022
Toll Free (844) 2REDEEM (273-3336)

Redemption Press is honored to present this title in partnership with the author. The views expressed or implied in this work are those of the author. Redemption Press provides our imprint seal representing design excellence, creative content and high quality production.

The ultimate design, content, editorial accuracy, and views expressed or implied in this work are those of the author. No part of this publication may be reproduced, stored in a retrieval system, or transmitted in any way by any means—electronic, mechanical, photocopy, recording, or otherwise—without the prior permission of the copyright holder, except as provided by USA copyright law.

Unless otherwise noted, all Scriptures are taken from the *New American Standard Bible*, 1960, 1962, 1963, 1968, 1971, 1972, 1973, 1975, 1977 by the Lockman Foundation.

Scripture references marked ASV are taken from the *American Standard Version* of the Holy Bible first published in 1901 by Thomas Nelson and Sons.

Scripture references marked KJV are taken from the *King James Version* of the Bible.

Scripture references marked NIV are taken from the *Holy Bible, New International Version*®, NIV®. Copyright © 1973, 1978, 1984 by the New York International Bible Society. Used by permission of Zondervan. Bible Publishers. All rights reserved worldwide.

ISBN 13: 978-1-63232-252-4 (Print)
978-1-63232-254-8 (ePub)
978-1-63232-255-5 (Mobi)
Library of Congress Catalog Card Number: 2015933752

Dedication

To all the New Generation who are seeking to know God, and to live for Him.

And, especially to my grandchildren who have inspired me to share my knowledge of the One who loves us so much that He, the Lord God, has provided us with a Savior who wants to rescue us.

Contents

Introduction..ix

Chapter One: God's Acceptance.................... 13
Chapter Two: Making the Right Choice............. 19
Chapter Three: God's Individual Plan 25
Chapter Four: God's Expectations 31
Chapter Five: Hope for Today 37
Chapter Six: Answered Prayer..................... 43
Chapter Seven: Two Sides of Suffering 49
Chapter Eight: The Intended Abundant Life 55
Chapter Nine: Top Priorities 61
Chapter Ten: Composure in Difficulties............ 69
Chapter Eleven: Overcoming Negative Thoughts...... 75
Chapter Twelve: Important Encounters 81
Chapter Thirteen: Resting in Jesus................ 87

Chapter Fourteen: Never Compromise the Truth........ 93
Chapter Fifteen: Faith, Our Support 99
Chapter Sixteen: Jesus Wept....................... 105
Chapter Seventeen: The Beauty of God 111
Chapter Eighteen: Priests of God 117
Chapter Nineteen: Spiritual Gifts................... 123
Chapter Twenty: Our Weaknesses 129
Chapter Twenty-One: Inexpressible Joy 135
Chapter Twenty-Two: Studying God's Word 141
Chapter Twenty-Three: Believers Matter 147
Chapter Twenty-Four: Walking With God............ 153
Chapter Twenty-Five: Remaining Faithful 161
Chapter Twenty-Six: Being Truthful................. 167
Chapter Twenty-Seven: Visible Glory................ 173
Chapter Twenty-Eight: Our Calling................. 179
Chapter Twenty-Nine: The Best Defense 185
Chapter Thirty: The New Year..................... 191
Chapter Thirty-One: Time for Review 195
Chapter Thirty-Two: Worthy of Praise............... 201

Introduction

There are two distinct valleys mentioned in the Bible to which we can all personally relate. The valley of Baca is the one most of us are familiar with from experience, for most of us have walked through troubling circumstances often in life. Baca is the valley of weeping, suffering, and mourning; a place where tears flow due to the difficulties of life we are called to bear. But the Scripture in Psalm 84:6 declares that we do "pass through" this valley. So we know that there will be a rainbow at the end of our difficult times, when we reach the other side of sorrow. For although suffering is a hard area in life to be in, the valley of Baca is noted in the sacred writings of God as not being our permanent residence, for we pass through to the other side.

Perhaps this is the same valley mentioned by King David in Psalm 23:4, as he refers to walking through the valley of the shadow of death. Although his enemies cast a long shadow over him, David trusted God. In those difficult moments, he expressed his confidence in the Good Shepherd to walk with him through the valley he refers to as a place of deep darkness.

In such challenging times as he faced, David knew that the Lord would provide all he needed and also would comfort him by His presence, for David, the king, was always aware of the Lord's nearness.

The second valley mentioned above that comes to mind is the valley of Berachah (2 Chronicles 20:26), known as a glorious place of victory brought about by God. The Israelite people called it the valley of Berachah or "blessing." Here the people had learned that the battles of life belong to God. For the only way we can win in our struggles is through God's strength. Our fears and weaknesses limit what we can do; and we need to ask God daily for His help to walk us through each valley we are called to cross. When we admit we are powerless against our enemies and invite God to be our protector and provider, He will turn our defeats into victories.

God has not only revealed in the Scriptures who He is as our Creator, but also that His nature is unchanging love and that He cares about our lives. So we find in His Word that He will willingly lead us through life's hard times and guide our every step, when we turn to Him for answers.

In the following pages, practical counsel and heavenly wisdom from God's Word can be gleaned with the help of the Holy Spirit's direction. There can be found God's principles, guidelines, and solutions. I cannot emphasis this enough, for the Bible is *truth* from above. God's remedies work! The Scriptures contain answers to life's most difficult questions. This wisdom from heaven makes a difference in how we confront daily life. God does not want us to struggle alone!

The questions chosen to appear in this particular book are ones often asked by true seekers. Each question has an answer found in the Holy Word. As you read, truly meditate on what

God has shared and ask Him to help you apply His wisdom to your life. There isn't a need that arises that God hasn't already given His guidance in the Scriptures on how to handle that need. Directly or indirectly, His principles do apply. He delights in helping us fulfill His plans for our lives by removing the obstacles, or assisting us to overcome them, as we seek to do His will. God will supply the answers when we acknowledge our dependence on Him and turn in prayer, seeking His guidance. Enjoy your journey, dear reader, as you search for His answers, knowing that God will lift you from the valley of Baca—weeping—into the valley of Berachah—blessing.

Chapter One

GOD'S ACCEPTANCE

We all long to be accepted. Being included is a basic need of all human beings. Whether we recognize that need or not, a desire to be accepted is part of our make-up, which is instilled by God. We often wonder what the requirement is to be included in a family, the community, or especially by God? *Do I belong?* With our acceptance of God into our hearts, we find we are truly accepted by God Himself.

"This is My beloved Son, in whom I am well-pleased."
(Matthew 3:17)

Q: How do we know God loves us just as we are and desires a relationship with us that can truly change our lives?

A: The month of February is normally a time when people turn their thoughts to the subject of love—the romantic, physical love of a couple who seem totally devoted to each other and desire to spend their lives together. But, people may not necessarily consider the love of God that has been revealed through His Son, Christ Jesus. This comes to mind instead mostly during the Christmas or Easter holidays. While a relationship may start with strong feelings of affection, a truly God-centered couple will move on from romantic love to the deeper kind of caring that is called *agape* love in the Scriptures (1 Corinthians 13:13). Agape love is not self-centered desire, but rather the sacrificial passion and effort to put others before self. This kind of deep love is God's compassion toward us even though we are sinners in His sight. Our comprehension of such love becomes stronger and more intimate, as we begin to experience Christ's presence in our lives.

While here on earth, Jesus gave us the *greatest example* of agape love. His whole life was centered on revealing our heavenly Father, who is love (Colossians 1:15, Hebrews 1:3, 1 John 4:8). This is a very deep concept to be contemplated by us. Every action or deed performed by Jesus was centered on revealing the radiant love, the consistent compassion, and the awesome desire of God for a relationship with us. Comprehending such love means we finally grasp that His great compassion moved Him to action so we could experience love firsthand.

Wherever He went, Jesus taught the will of God by proclaiming the gospel message of truth to those who were spiritually blind. He also showed great compassion for the sick and spent endless hours touching, healing, and restoring *hope* in the downtrodden and brokenhearted. Jesus continued also to cast out the demons that were afflicting many, and He restored peace to nature during certain storms that created fear among His followers. The Lord's whole life demonstrated real agape *love in action*, and His willingness to accept sinners, who need to be close to Him.

Once, overlooking the city of Jerusalem, the Lord evaluated the situation and prayed for the people's needs. Jesus felt that day a tremendous weight of sorrow, and He wept for those who were rejecting His offer of peace between God and man. Yet, Jesus endured this personal rejection out of His great love for the lost, and He fulfilled His ministry to set the captives, who believed in Him, free from their sins. Christ's life demonstrated God reaching out to us. Jesus did that while we were still sinners by revealing God's willingness to accept us back into His family through the Lord Jesus as the only way.

Jesus was deeply concerned for both the pressing crowds and the individual. His ministry of love is reflected by His actions of feeding the hungry thousands and closely noting the widow's meager offering in the temple. The Lord pointed out to His disciples that her gift truly came from a devoted heart, since she did not give from her surplus, but she gave all that she had (Luke 21:2-3). To those who sought Him, Jesus consistently extended forgiveness, offered encouragement, and showed unfailing love. He readily accepted those troubled souls who came to Him and He fed them both physically and spiritually. The individual mattered and matters to Him.

The apostle John made a summary statement in his gospel regarding the Lord's life here on earth that says Jesus did much more than is recorded (John 20:30). John declared that there were many other "signs" Jesus performed for people's benefit. The disciples were His witnesses to those events and deeds that revealed His deep love. So numerous were they that those events remain unknown to us. Jesus cared and showed His deep affection for others as He walked among the people. God still cares for us even in our worst condition. He cares enough to want to transform our lives—remaking us into better people.

Christ's main purpose for being on earth was fulfilled at the climax of His life on the cross (1 John 3:16). He had come to save sinners by paying the price for their redemption and to lift all mankind out of the devastating bondage of sin. No deeper love can be extended than the giving of one's life so that others can benefit for all eternity. Jesus did that on Calvary with moving compassion.

Yes, God loves us even when we are sinners and not pleasing to Him. He cared enough to give His Son as atonement for our sins, the very Son in whom He was pleased, and the only Son who offers the chance to lost people to be redeemed. Jesus, in His marvelous heart-rending love, showed us the way through His sacrifice. We can truly know God's love by just trusting and accepting Jesus, for God accepts us.

> Does God accept us who are sinners?
> He has demonstrated His willingness by giving His Son.
> Acceptance, though, is a two-way event.
> Receiving such marvelous love needs an open heart.
> Reach out with joy to the love God offers, and become one of His children by His openness to include even the lost.

On the first meeting of my soon-to-be mother-in-law, I felt accepted. No one could enter her home without being greeted with a big, warm hug, and you could never leave her residence without the same kind of strong embrace being given to you as you departed.

Elizabeth was a woman who loved deeply and completely. Over the years, Mom Gorham proved her love was true with consistency and encouragement. In the latter years of her life before her death at one hundred, she repeatedly told me on my visits that I was her daughter, and not to let anyone tell me differently. During the thirty-eight years we had together, Mom G. became to me the mother I never knew in my early years. She made great big dinners and we shared long talks at our gatherings, and our intimacy deepened over the years as we traveled together or just visited. She openly accepted me in every way.

In the late 1800s, Elizabeth was raised on an Idaho farm by her grandparents who were not the kind of people who showed affection or demonstrated deep feelings. Mom had come away from that experience feeling unloved, so I'm sure that motivated her to show strongly how she really felt to her own children and to others. Some people by nature are more demonstrative with their affections than others, but no one more naturally than Mom Gorham.

Almighty God bases His acceptance on our relationship with Christ and what Jesus did on the cross as our substitute. If we accept Jesus and His sacrifice, then we have accepted the only way back to God. The Lord Jesus opened the door, and God accepts those who follow Christ.

God sees us through the cleansing blood of Jesus, and that never changes. Once accepted on those grounds, because we believe in Jesus, we remain accepted. Though we may stumble and fall, God will clearly accept us back into His loving embrace when we ask for His forgiveness. As with Mom Gorham's love, God's love is unchanging, consistent, and faithful to the end.

Review:

Being accepted is a great thing. Being truly loved is something that we naturally long for. Being made to feel you belong and are wanted is vital in our relationships and our life experiences. The same is true in our relationship with God. We desire to know that we belong and that God openly accepts those who seek Him.

Closing Remarks:
God demonstrated His love.
He offered a way for us to belong.
True love draws people in and is not selfish.
Christ's life was love in action.
Real love is sacrificial passion for others.

Chapter Two

MAKING THE RIGHT CHOICE

Free will is a part of our nature, for God established this as a trait within each individual. This feature allows us to make choices unhampered and freely. We can think and act on our own, uncontrolled by others or divine imposition. What we do with this gift establishes consequences—either good ones or bad ones for us to live with.

"Come now, and let us reason together," says the Lord.
(Isaiah 1:18)

Q: What does it mean to have a free will?

A: At creation, all humanity was given the ability to make choices in any situation. When a decision becomes necessary or a choice must be made, human beings have a free will that is not hampered or coerced by God. A person can think or act as he or she wishes. What we do and how we react is connected to the decisions we make. This freedom conferred by God to us means there is opportunity for unrestricted action on our part. What does this truly mean?

God, our Creator, has made each of us with the ability to be a self-determining being, acting in accordance with our own will. We have a mind and the ability to think. We are not robots who have no say in our destiny. Human beings can choose to be in line with God's divine laws or in conflict with them. The option remains open to following God's will or our own. We can be obedient to God or rebellious against Him.

We live in a sinful, fallen world, not the world that God created originally that was perfect and good. Man's choices over the years have created a corrupt world in opposition to God. Individuals who have no relationship with God, or fail to heed His advice, often choose what is wrong, bringing consequences on themselves and others. Our choices do bring consequences— good ones and bad ones. The reality can come immediately or later on in life, which sometimes causes people to think they got away with their decisions. People often enlarge the aftermath of their deeds by becoming angry and bitter at the results, inflicting more wrong on others. Life then becomes a vicious cycle of imposing more evil and pain on those nearby, usually the ones they have the most affection for.

When a man or woman is facing the consequences of his or her behavior, he or she tends to blame existing conditions, the influence of others, or some specific circumstance as being responsible for what has happened. Some people even readily blame God for the transpiring events, rather than assuming responsibility themselves for what they have done. But, the biblical concept as to why we find ourselves in difficult situations has to do with choice. Our choices matter!

In the beginning, man was created in God's image with perfect freedom. Man's original condition before the fall in the garden was excellent (Genesis 1:26-27). Adam and Eve were sinless, but had a free will (Genesis 2:16-17). When they fell from God's grace by disobedience, both became in bondage to sin. The consequences of sin by our first parents resulted in human beings inheriting a fallen nature (Genesis 3:8). But man still had the ability to choose. This change left human beings in need of God's grace and the Holy Spirit to restore them spiritually. Throughout Scriptures, God's Word teaches that man has been invested with the capacity to choose between obedience and disobedience. A man or a woman can discern between right actions and sinful ones despite the damage done by the original fall. The human free will remains intact.

In the Scriptures, an example is given when Cain slew his brother Abel. This event illustrates one's free will in action. Cain's mental distress before was noticeable to God by his facial expression, because Cain's mood had visibly changed his countenance. God spoke to him before the killing of his brother, warning Cain to control his feelings, but Cain failed to do so. Disregarding God's instructions, he slew his brother (Genesis 4:4-8), which brought life-changing consequences. Cain lived the rest of his days separated from God and on a destructive course.

Freedom to make choices is always allowed by God. Our will remains under our own control, but a real relationship with God is only obtainable by our surrendering our will and living in obedient fellowship with Him. Surrendering our will to God's control does not limit our joy in life, but rather yielding really enhances our joy.

By His righteousness, Christ made it possible for all believers to be redeemed and willingly submit their wills to Him (Ephesians 1:7, 4:20-24). Our condition when redeemed by

Christ is then governed by a newfound freedom. This means Jesus freed us from the predisposition of even the compulsion to sin by extending the gift of His Holy Spirit to indwell each believer. The power of all believers to choose between right and wrong is enhanced by the living presence of the Holy Spirit in us, if we allow Him to be our helper. By His grace, we can make the right choice. We no longer have to "carry out the desire of the flesh," because we have the Holy Spirit's power to sustain us (Galatians 5:16). The conscience becomes shaped to the will of God by the presence of the Holy Spirit within each person, but only when the Spirit is allowed to function.

The apostle Paul states, "It was for freedom that Christ set us free; therefore keep standing firm and do not be subject again to a yoke of slavery" (Galatians 5:1). That is real freedom! Peter said, "Act as free men, and do not use your freedom as a covering for evil, but use it as bondslaves of God" (1 Peter 2:16). Under God's yoke, we can experience an awesome freedom that was unknown before. We can follow God's way in our walk through this life by letting go the control of all matters to Him who knows what is best. We have to choose to do right, not wrong, and with the Lord's help we can overcome the desire to sin.

> God has given men and women a free will.
> What we do with it remains in our control.
> Using our free will wisely means we consult God,
> and heed His advice by submitting our will to His.
> Allowing the Holy Spirit to guide our decisions
> is the wise way to go.
> God offers the best, why not choose
> to do things His way?

God chose my husband, Bert, for me, and told me His decision the first night we met. Bert seemed nice enough, open and friendly, but I felt no real attraction to the man that evening. Shortly after that meeting in March at an archery club gathering, I learned that he left the area for several months to visit his sister in Texas.

I went on with my life that included mostly working in an office, and getting to know a few of my sister's friends, for I was new to the area. I found an apartment downtown, bought an old Chev coupe for transportation, and located what was to be my home church for the next seven years. Not once during my settling-in time did I wonder what had happened to Bert or even want to see him.

In the following months as my life moved on at its own pace, I dated three different guys, and I was attracted to another local cowboy, who seemed not to notice I existed.

That fall Bert and I met again at the archery range, and this time he asked me if I wanted to go to a movie, but I declined his offer. We went peacefully our separate ways. Six months later, we both attended an archery club Valentine's Day event that turned our relationship around. Somehow, we clicked and danced the whole night, mostly together. Until then, I had not taken God's instructions seriously or followed up in any way on His announcement that I would marry Bert. From Valentine's Day on, we dated often and came to the agreement that we would marry in May of that same year. We spent the next twenty-seven years together finding out that God knew what was best for us. We were right for each other, and Bert's sudden death left me extremely grateful for the time we had together.

Following God's instructions was the best decision I ever made. His pronouncement still allowed me to choose. I was not in any way forced, and I am very glad I listened to my Lord. Bert was a caring, gentle man with good principles and great concern for others, who also gave his heart fully to God and loved serving Him.

My free will was never hindered by God's proclamation that I would marry Bert. By accepting God's choice, I discovered a great love that remained faithful and was best for me.

Review:

We are self-determining beings, who have a say in our destination. Obedience or disobedience is our choice, since God desires our response to be out of love. Good or bad consequences will result depending on whom we follow. Real freedom and real joy comes from letting God have control.

Closing Remarks:

God gave us a free will.
He desires a relationship with us.
We can reason things out with the help of the Holy Spirit.
Our choices matter!

Chapter Three

GOD'S INDIVIDUAL PLAN

Understanding our gifts and talents helps us discern the plan God has for each of our lives. He has a task for us to complete, and by fulfilling this service, we will find total satisfaction and contentment. Beyond finding meaning for life here, we are being prepared for eternal life with Him in heaven. Understanding God's plan for our lives and not wasting the time He gives us goes way beyond just working at a job.

> "For I know the plans that I have for you,"
> declares the Lord,
> "Plans for welfare and not for calamity,
> to give you a future and a hope."
> (Jeremiah 29:11)

Q: As a Christian, are you concerned that you have failed to fulfill God's plan and purpose for your life?

A: Often we are unsure of the direction God desires for our lives to take. We may stumble along on a course that we have chosen questioning if we have made the right decisions. As the days seem to fly away and the years advance rapidly, we may wonder if the path we've taken has been pleasing to God. And, we often feel we have failed.

In the book of Proverbs, a father is speaking to his son and emphasizing the importance of trusting the Lord over attempting to handle life by his own understanding (Proverbs 3:5.6). This is sound advice. When we start any project, to be successful we must consider all the possibilities, evaluate the total situation, and estimate the cost of the venture (Luke 14:31-33). God has given us the ability to reason and plan our lives, while setting the goals and the objectives we may desire to reach. But, only when our ways are committed to the Lord's way, will God establish the means of fulfilling them (Proverbs 16:1-3; 7-9). In other words when we acknowledge God, He will create a straight course to proceed on and the provisions to fulfill the tasks. But He needs to be a part of the groundwork preparations and planning at the very beginning.

The Lord Jesus really wants us to understand that a truly fulfilled life doesn't consist of what possessions we acquire or the positions that we may obtain. A life that is rich will be one that enhances our relationship to our Creator (Luke 12:13-21). Our first priority should be to cultivate our relationship with God through our personal association with Christ Jesus, His Son. Our productive years will then be the result of God blessing our lives as we serve Him.

Whatever plans we make that are done without consulting God can lead to failure and a sense of not achieving the pursuit of God's calling on our lives. In the book of Luke, the Lord revealed how a rich man plotted to build more storage for his abundant crops, but he did so without seeking God's advice on the matter (Luke 12:18). While he was extremely successful, he had ignored the spiritual relationship necessary for a complete life. Without our divine connection, our spiritual part remains damaged and incomplete. In the case of the rich man this was permanently so, for he died that same night. His decision to build more barns without consulting God for what He wanted him to accomplish was foolish. In the end, his choice left him without an eternal relationship with God. When we are not in tune with God, we fall short and lack personal satisfaction and experience discontentment in our lives. This choice can affect us eternally also.

Those who devotedly seek God's advice and direction as a regular manner of approaching life will find His plan, and they will be able to fulfill it (Proverbs 16:9). God has promised that He will instruct those seeking His avenues of service (Psalm 32:8). Jesus will meet us where we are in life (John 21:15-19). He then will help us find our way. The Lord stands beside us on the path to assist and encourage us in our actions (Acts 23:11, 26:15-18). The indwelling presence of the Holy Spirit makes known to the Christian what steps are right in accordance with God's will (Psalm 143:10). The very love of God for us will direct our course, when coupled with His grace and applied to our lives by our asking.

When sent to find a wife for Abraham's son Isaac, Abraham's servant prayed to God these words, "O Lord, the God of my master Abraham, please grant me success today" (Genesis 24:12). When his search was completed the servant also wisely acknowledged God's guidance (Genesis 24:27). The apostle James declared, "If the Lord wills, we will live and also do this or that" (James 4:15). May asking God for directions be our banner in all of life; then we can rest assured that we are on the right path. The plan God has for us individually will become clear and be one that we can fulfill.

How do we know God's plan for our lives?
By acknowledging our Creator's promise for guidance we know.
Seeking His will for our decisions must be our top priority.
God loves being included.
He desires only the best for us,
and He will direct our paths when we turn to Him.

I came from a rural setting, and attended a small country school. We had good teachers, but no elaborate educational opportunities, only the basics. So when I graduated from high school, I had no real idea what direction I should go in life. I had high marks as a student, been cast in leadership roles, acted in several dramatic plays, and had developed lasting friendships, but I was left wondering what I would do in life.

In those days, women were more destined to marry and raise a family, with no thought of a personal career. Few were lawyers, doctors, or business owners. The woman's role was to mother her children and lovingly care for the man's "castle." That was her career. So I felt that I would eventually marry in a few years, but I remained unsure of what to do in the meantime. Deep inside, I wondered what other talents I might have and should develop.

I worked for a while as a nurse's aide and loved those days, and then I went to work in an office, as I was good at math and most secretarial procedures. But, my heart wasn't satisfied. I seemed to have an empty spot, even though I enjoyed the work and the people connected with the steel shop where I was employed. So ten years after my high school graduation, I enrolled in a Bible college to further my education, as I felt led to do so by God.

I had married and by that time had two sons whom I adored. I loved my husband, Bert, and we were good for each other, and I still felt my first and foremost job was to be his wife and to mother his children. While my husband and I wanted to become missionaries to Australia, after two years of planning, we discovered that our plans were not God's plan for us. Even though during those two years, events seemed to say that the door was open for us to go in that direction.

During those days, I was terribly frustrated, since I was doing the same routine things I did before I started Bible college. I washed the family clothes and ironed them, made beds and cooked meals for five daily, cleaned house and entertained family and friends, yet something was lacking in my life. The only time in my existence that I got mad at God was during those days of trying to discover in what area of service I was meant to function. I felt that I didn't need further education to take care of my home and family. Finding the Lord's plan for my life and His intended path seemed impossible.

Slowly a different route opened for me as I did volunteer work for the college and eventually became a vocational counselor there, helping students find employment. God directed my husband and me toward doing home Bible studies all over the Puget Sound area and working with different churches that had building needs. Gradually, I became a teacher of His Word, and advanced to counseling others in all areas from premarital to crisis counseling. I had found my place in God's kingdom and discovered that deep personal satisfaction that had been missing in those earlier years. God had given me real purpose on the home front, not in some far distant country where others might be called to serve. After twenty-seven years of marriage, my husband passed away. Then I could understand clearly that God had been preparing me to continue doing the work of counseling, for which I was best suited, after the man I had loved was gone.

Our Creator has individual plans for us. Those plans may or may not include a mate. His plans may mean we travel all over the world, or simply stay at home. The Lord always strives to put us where we can serve to the best of our ability. He loves us and wants us to share in His joy and contentment, even as we work.

Review:

Our goals should reflect God's plan and purpose for our lives. We should include God in the groundwork. Plans that do not consider God's calling are foolish and will fail. The wise servant will acknowledge God's guidance. The banner over our lives should be asking God and trusting Him to lead.

Closing Remarks:

Not wasting our time is important.
The Holy Spirit makes known what steps are right.
God puts us where we can use our talents and abilities best.
Out of love for us God directs our course.

Chapter Four

GOD'S EXPECTATIONS

God holds high expectations for His children. Throughout the Scriptures, God has firmly expressed the need of obedience in the lives of His people. He has set us free from sin so we may come into His presence by our renewed righteousness. Our rebirth through Christ covers us with His righteousness, but we are to maintain our relationship with God by striving to be holy.

> And God is able to make all grace abound to you,
> so that always having all sufficiency in everything,
> you may have an abundance for every good deed.
> (2 Corinthians 9:8)

Q: Are you involved in a period of intense spiritual questioning? Or have you ever wondered what God expects of His children?

A: God offers the answer to the questions often asked by His people by inspiring the apostle Peter to instruct them to live godly lives. In the book of 1 Peter, chapters 1-6, Peter conveys hope, comfort, and encouragement to those who stand firm in their faith. Speaking to Christians, the apostle refers to them as being *obedient* children (1 Peter 1:14). We must obey and entrust our whole lives to our faithful Creator to be successful in our walks with God (1 Peter 4:19). Peter enhances this by encouraging them to be *holy* in all aspects of their lives (1 Peter 1:14,15). God simply requires us to be spiritually whole and to do this through His own grace.

Further, Peter instructs Christians to remember we are God's chosen people, who are called "out of darkness into His marvelous light" (1 Peter 2:9). What an incredible thing to be so transformed! Called from the dark side of life to the bright side, as God's people we must lay aside the negative things of this world (especially fleshly lusts and desires), and strive toward excellent behavior and doing good deeds that glorify God (1 Peter 2:12).

While journeying through this old world toward our heavenly home, Christians must be nourished, guided, and strengthened by God's Word and from fellowship with other believers (1 Peter 2:2). To do so, Peter conveys that we need to long for the pure Word, while striving to follow in the footsteps of Jesus, who is our example (1 Peter 2:21).

While He walked among the people, Jesus was gracious, kind, compassionate, and helpful. As our "Shepherd and Guardian of our souls," He made it possible for us to live righteously (1 Peter 2:25). We now have before us Jesus Christ by whom we can model our behavior accordingly, for He never sinned, so we must concentrate on cultivating within ourselves "the imperishable quality of a gentle and quiet spirit" (1 Peter 3:4). By being sympathetic, kind, harmonious, brotherly, humble, speaking blessings to others, and zealous for good works (in our common family, the church), our inner person will reflect the very *love* of God (1 Peter 3:8). That is what God expects! The world around us will then see us living the will of God out in our lives.

God spoke strict instructions to the Israelites on what He expected of them.

> And now, Israel, what does the Lord your God require from you, but to fear the Lord your God, to walk in all His ways and love Him, and to serve the Lord your God with all your heart and with all your soul and to keep the Lord's commandments and His statutes which I am commanding you today for your good?
> (Deuteronomy 10:12-13)

God further expresses His desire in Micah 6:8 and Ezekiel 18:5-9 for us to consider.

By accepting Christ as our Lord and Savior, the Holy Spirit will bring into our lives love, joy, peace, patience, kindness, goodness, faithfulness, gentleness, and self-control—the fruit of the Spirit (1 Peter 4:2, Galatians 5:22-23). As Christians, we must work to develop these traits as an obvious part of our lives. These abilities become possible when each person truly establishes Christ as sovereign ruler in his or her heart (2 Peter 3:15). In other words, as Christians, we must allow Christ alone to rule our lives. Each one should give to Him respect and loyal service. As good stewards of whatever special gifts God has entrusted to us, we will then desire to "love and honor all men" (2 Peter 2:17), and to "seek peace and pursue it" (2 Peter 3:11).

Even in times of suffering, we should remember the *joy* that lies ahead when we will receive the promised inheritance from

Christ Jesus in heaven. God expects us to be loving, obedient, and holy children, but He, Himself, is the source of all the grace necessary to accomplish this. God has never intended for His children to handle life alone. So, we must lay aside the spiritual questioning that may be troubling us and just be obedient to God, and the rest will fall into its proper place.

> God does have strong expectations of His children.
> He has stated those guidelines in the Scriptures.
> While high requirements,
> they are possible to attain by His grace which He freely gives.
> Believers are not expected to do things alone.

Living the Christian life reflects back to God His love and it shows others that same love, without any selfishness. I often think of a couple of women I've known who could do this very thing so naturally, and seemingly without effort. There was just genuine warmth in their voice as they spoke, and even in the smallest details, their loving action and concern showed.

One of these ladies, Reathel, I got to know quite well over the years, while the other was more an acquaintance from brief encounters at church each Sunday for only a few years. But, I sensed in each of these women great affection that was hard to explain, and something I felt lacking within myself toward others.

They both were sincere and real, showing a spiritual purity in their lives that I had not yet obtained. They seemed to accept people no matter what their circumstances might be. People were important to them.

After I moved to Washington State in 1955, my only contact with Reathel was by mail. It was too expensive those days to make long-distance calls, so for years we wrote back and forth. Her love and concern was in every line. That left a lasting impression on my life, for she was one who showed deep interest in how my life was progressing.

Allowing the love of God to reach out to others through us brings us a step closer to being holy, as God desires. Showing kindness, even in a handshake or giving others a few minutes of our time, models a life more like Christ's. He made time for people. God expects our lives to be real, pure, and humble with nothing phony displayed—just sincere love! This was what I was witnessing in the lives of those two Christian women.

Review:

As children of God, we are to strive to be holy. We can accomplish this by being obedient to God. Our desire should be to glorify God with our lives. Following the example of Christ Jesus, we should be gracious, kind, helpful, and compassionate. By cultivating the gifts of the Holy Spirit in our lives, we will grow more like Him. By reflecting the love of God, we are modeling Jesus' behavior and God's will.

Closing Remarks:

God expects His children to love others.
God demands that we humbly serve others for our good.
Making Christ the sovereign ruler of our lives is essential.
God's grace is sufficient to aid us in our holy walk.

Chapter Five

HOPE FOR TODAY

Hope is a necessary ingredient in life. This marvelous and obtainable belief inspires us to go on no matter what may be assailing us in life. Trusting God brings with it the profound assurance that He is in control and He will protect and assist our ventures in life. Hope is confidence that the end results will be favorable based on a solid foundation of faith in God. In God's Word we find encouragement and hope.

> This hope we have as an anchor of the soul,
> a hope both sure and steadfast.
> (Hebrews 6:19)

Q: Can Christians experience real hope when our daily expectations grow dim by circumstances in our everyday lives?

A: Webster's Dictionary defines hope as, "A desire with the expectation of obtaining what is desired, or belief that a desire is obtainable." In the Scriptures, hope means trust and a confident expectation of a future reality. In the New Testament, a joyful and contented expectation of eternal salvation is offered the Christian—a reality that is obtainable in the future based on Christ's work (Acts 23:6, 26:7; Romans 5:4). The second coming of the Lord is our blessed hope, for God has promised Christians a glorious inheritance and future home with Him in heaven (Titus 2:13).

In times of suffering now, Christians can hope for better days, and be glad that our time is short here compared to all eternity. God offers Christians a "living hope" in Christ Jesus (1 Peter 1:3), not just a future hope obtained only in heaven, but an active hope now available in this present life. People need to realize this living hope is available to sustain us in life's present situations. Jesus promised to be with His followers all the time, and He does so by His Spirit living in believers from the day they accept Him as Lord of their lives (John 14:16-23). Even when the path of life becomes rough, the Christian who has confidence in God, can maintain a brighter outlook on life, because God is always faithful. He will be there to help us (Hebrews 13:5-6).

Our hope is grounded in God's Word and God's promises, and especially in Christ Jesus who makes God's grace available to us. The bad situations in life do not have the final say. By His grace we can endure. Psalm 146:5 (KJV) reads, "Happy is he . . . whose hope is in the Lord his God." Note the personal relationship between the psalmist and God. The believer has a private and intimate relationship with God based on His love for us, and His determination to restore us into His fellowship. God loves us and wants our love in return—that's personal. As Christians we have reason to believe in the fulfillment of our expectations that are based on God's Word, for Jesus Christ Himself is our hope (Colossians 1:27; 1 Timothy 1:1).

In the Old Testament, words like safety, security, trust, and refuge all were expressions of hope based on man's relationship to God. God is the source, the very fountain, and the ultimate security of all believers' expectations. Through Jesus we have knowledge of God's love, goodness, grace, faithfulness, and greatness. God is "the God of hope" (Romans 15:13). God wants His people to believe and hope. By the power of God's Holy Spirit, we can abound in hope, joy, and peace. Realizing that we do not have to carry the burdens alone, nor solve the problems in our own strength, relieves the stress and brings us extreme joy.

The non-believer has no real certainty about how to handle life based on no absolute in which to trust. In contrast, the Christian has a clear and definite hope based on Jesus Christ and His Word. As Christians, we can face life with confidence no matter what may come.

Daily, the Christian needs to emphasize the *hope* we are offered by God, for that becomes our anchor in life. No matter what valley we find ourselves in, we do have hope we will pass on through the rough terrain. The Word of God emphasizes we do not remain in the valley of sorrow, but the Lord walks with us through the deepest hollows of life (Psalm 23:4). What a comfort to know our stay in each difficulty will be temporary! Soon the path will lift us from the valley of despair and destruction and bring us new life. While the times may vary for each situation to be overcome, the hard times won't last.

All human beings need hope to function well in life.
To have a working sense of hope we need a relationship.
For such certainty there must be a strong
link between God and man.

> Confidence in Almighty God is our anchor.
> When we are connected to God, He becomes our source.
> Through Him a believer lacks none of the necessities.
> When distress comes by various trials, we can have hope in God to be there for us.

A friend recently shared the news about a tragic accidental death of a family member that happened because one inexperienced family member attempted to follow the instructions of another and lost control of some large equipment. The life of one was lost and the other's life was shattered with the lasting memory of their unintentional actions. Yet, there remained hope in this terrible situation, because the deceased person knew Christ Jesus as his Lord.

The lost mate was well known in his community as a Christian, and many people came out to his funeral to show their love. He had deep faith in what the Lord Jesus had done for him, and because of his faith this man could be in God's presence after he lost his life in such a sorrowful manner. There would be in the future a reunion between the one left behind and the one who went first to heaven. Hope can fade quickly in such hard moments, but from God's perspective, with faith comes hope.

Those types of sad moments can have a completely different outcome, depending on whether the person is a non-believer or a believer in Christ. We never know when death will overtake us or how, so we need to be prepared to stand before God and say with joy, "Jesus is my Lord, because I believe in Him and have accepted Him as my Savior. Jesus is my hope."

Review:

Hope is an essential aspect of life. Real hope is based on God's revealed truth in His Word. We need confidence that the end results will be favorable in our situations. Based on Christ's redemptive work, we have hope for now and all eternity. Christ has opened the door to God who supplies His people with grace to overcome.

Closing Remarks:

Real hope brings safety, security, and refuge to those who trust God.
God is the source of grace, strength, and hope.
Christians can face life with confidence.
We can abound in our hope in Christ Jesus.
Difficulties won't last.
There is real hope in God.

Chapter Six

ANSWERED PRAYER

Our prayers are important to God. They are retained in heaven as a message of fragrant incense. To God they are sweet-smelling messages of love from us. Not only does God listen to our requests, and Christ mediates in the Lord Almighty's presence on our behalf, but God graciously answers in ways that benefit us. Our prayers open the way to access God's grace and mercy—things vital to our life.

> Be anxious for nothing, but in everything by prayer
> and supplication with thanksgiving
> let your requests be made known to God.
> (Philippians 4:6)

Q: How can we recognize God's answer to our prayers?

A: Prayer is the means by which Christians take an active part in determining their course in life. Each prayer we extend to God should be based on our own real desire to know His will in *all* matters. As Christians, prayer is our lifeline to God. The Lord Jesus has given us the responsibility of asking, seeking, and knocking at the throne of grace for help. When we do follow His instructions, God promises He will help us find, receive, and discover a solution by opening the way of righteousness and giving His good gifts to help us (Matthew 7:7-11). God alone brings the pieces of any "puzzle" together and makes common sense out of what appears to us to be a real mess. Nothing is unimportant to God or impossible for Him. The Lord delights in being involved in every aspect of our lives, when we turn things over to Him. Our prayers open God's pathway that leads us through any conflict or need.

Each hour of the day Christians are in the holy presence of our all-knowing and all-powerful God, who is omnipresent (Psalm 139). He is busy confirming His presence in our lives with "signs, wonders, and miracles," even as Jesus did while on earth as He ministered to His disciples and others (John 20:30). Because He is sovereign Lord, our Father in heaven knows what our needs are even before we ask Him (Matthew 6:8). So when we pray, God makes it possible to accomplish the impossible, something we should always remember (Matthew 19:26).

Sometimes when we pray, we tend to overlook the obvious that God has already given the answer in His Holy Word. Whatever the subject, we need to search the Scriptures first, knowing that God is not the author of confusion (1 Corinthians 14:33). Searching the Scriptures can save us time, energy, and bring about a solution faster. If He has already spoken His will on the matter, God's desire will not change, and His established way offers the peace we need.

Sometimes we are inclined to expect certain answers, yet God's answer to our prayers may not necessarily be what we desire or even believe is right for the situation. As an example, just before going to the cross, Christ prayed and asked that the course of His life be changed, if it were God's will. The answer God gave was that Christ Jesus still must die on the cross to gain victory over death by paying the price for our sins. God answers every prayer for our good, because He is good, but not necessarily as we desire (Deuteronomy 10:13). The Almighty offers what will fulfill the greatest purpose in furthering His kingdom. His answers are based on His awareness of the total picture regarding our life. The more God is glorified in life, the more others become aware of their Creator, which draws the lost back into a relationship with Him and enhances the lives of believers. The solution may take us through painful circumstances, but in the end it is best. Above all, the Lord desires what is best for us as individuals, and what will glorify Him as God.

When we submit our lives to God's will, we are blessed in awesome ways. In the Scriptures, a number of methods are revealed that indicate the astonishing answers that come from God.

- Visual events occurred at Jesus' baptism. While He prayed, heaven opened and the Holy Spirit descended upon the Lord (Luke 3:21, 22). Later in His ministry, Jesus went to the mountain to pray and "His face became different" and His clothing changed—a special visual happening that revealed His divine glory (Luke 9:29).
- Auditory incidents are also recorded in both the Old and New Testaments. Often God spoke to individuals, and His powerful, authoritative voice was heard (Acts 9:4-6). At both events mentioned above, God also spoke directly to the disciples, making His instructions clear regarding how they were to respond to Jesus.

- God promises His peace to those who present their requests before Him (Philippians 4:6-7). A deep sense of calmness comes from God and reassures the one praying that this is the right pathway for him or her to pursue. After one prays, a confidence deep within comes from God that the decision is right.
- Since prayer is a two-way communication between the Father and His child, we must strive to keep the connection unbroken by asking and listening for God's response. By using prayer often, recognizing God's answers becomes second nature to a Christian.

God may point out the answer to our prayer in His Holy Word, or in a sermon we hear, or by other means such as speaking directly to our hearts by the Holy Spirit. The words may be only for our ears and no one else's. His answers do bring a profound peace that we are on the right path. By listening well, we can discern God's answers.

> Prayer is vital.
> It becomes the lifeline between God and man.
> Nothing is unimportant to God.
> We can enter the throne room and converse
> with our Creator any time.
> No matter what the problem may be or the time of need,
> God considers our prayers as fragrant incense
> that is retained in heaven, deserving an answer.

When our daughter, Deborah, was in the hospital at the age of four with a skull fracture, the neurologist expressed his concern that the four holes they had drilled in her skull, as a way to remove pressure from her head, might not heal. He said by that age the human skull usually has stopped growing. Also he said she might be required to wear a helmet to protect her from fatal accidents at home or at school. So her dad and I and others prayed for her complete healing and protection.

I lived in a stressful state of concern after we brought her home from the hospital, as I heard no direct reply from God regarding those prayers. The Lord had shown me His deep concern for her condition while she was hospitalized, but I heard nothing more from Him once she came home. I could only trust He loved her and would protect her.

Six months later the doctor examined the holes and confirmed they had been miraculously healed. From his joyful expression, I knew this was a rare happening.

During those one hundred and eighty days, I watched over Deborah and continued to have my concern. In this quiet time with no direct reply from God on the matter, I felt that perhaps He was waiting to see if my faith in Him would falter or endure. In my heart, I knew the Lord was faithful for He had shown His faithfulness many times in the past, but this experience helped me to openly express it more to others. He answered the many prayers lifted up on Deb's behalf, in His way and in His timing.

Review:

Our prayers are our lifeline to God, and they are important enough to be retained in heaven. As His followers, Christ meditates on our behalf, and God answers in various ways—something He promised to do. Nothing is unimportant to Him or impossible for Him. God's answers though may be different from what we expect, but however, they are right and good.

Closing Remarks:
God loves us and listens to us.
Our prayers should be based on a desire to know His will.
By praying, we are asking God to take an active part.
Our course in life is best when God's purpose becomes clear.
Ask, seek, and find are all action words.

Chapter Seven

Two Sides of Suffering

Our growth in Christ comes often from having to endure some form of suffering. The pain and hardship causes us to turn to God and allow Him to function in our lives, transforming us. Our dependence on God is deepened, and our realization of His marvelous grace and love becomes a part then of our daily walk with the Almighty. God is the potter, who shapes our character with trials that deepens our faith in Him.

> But if when you do what is right and suffer for it you
> patiently endure it, this finds favor with God.
> (1 Peter 2:20)

Q: Why do Christians suffer?

A: God has an absolute ongoing claim upon our lives, since He has forgiven our sins and we have become a part of His family. We are His servants in a world full of lost, hurting people, who are often selfish and self-seeking, empty individuals who inflict suffering upon others, especially believers. So there will be specific times when we must stand for Christ and His truth—and thus we may suffer. For the Christian, suffering with and for Jesus is a part of being a disciple and a condition that brings us glorification by Him. But, there are two sides to this extreme sort of pain Christians encounter: one for the sake of the kingdom of God, and one for our own personal benefit that hones our character to be more like Christ (2 Corinthians 3:18).

Throughout His ministry, Jesus rebuked His disciples for a lack of faith and their stubbornness that hindered them from understanding the divine teachings He presented to them (Mark 16:14). They were concerned with their own expectations, desires, ambitions, and traditions. The disciples had to learn to lay aside those worldly things, for these wants kept them blinded to God's will. As part of the body of Christ, the Church, Christians must adjust their thinking as to their position in Christ and become true followers of the Lord. Jesus said that His followers would suffer and be persecuted, as He their master had, because non-believers oppose God and His teachings (John 15:20). Our position in Christ places us on the path of suffering.

The apostle Peter provides us with an example of what effort it often takes to become a real servant of Christ. Instead of lovingly supporting the Lord just before His death, Peter denied knowing Jesus. Although his behavior was understandable because of the human fear of possible hurt, Peter denied Christ as He predicted. That same night at Peter's third denial, he was brought to a point of brokenness by only the look in his Savior's eyes (Luke 22:61-62). In that moment, Peter saw himself as unworthy of Christ's love. But Peter's character was dramatically changed by his realization of the Savior's suffering and his part in it, something all believers need to realize for themselves. We all played a part in His suffering. When we acknowledge though how much we benefit from Christ's death, then we can willingly suffer while sharing the good news of His life. Our suffering then benefits the kingdom of God.

What is the foundation of our life? Do our actions conform to what we believe? Many times in life we go through the same breaking process that Peter had to endure. In those moments, God forces us to turn away from our own interests and see life from His perspective (John 15:5). When the pain becomes great, we become teachable and can grow spiritually (Job 40:4), and then the suffering benefits us personally.

Suffering is to be endured for a season; and God has promised to not allow more than we can tolerate. Each type of pain imposed on us can enhance our life, if we strive to determine why God allowed the suffering. The important thing to remember during those difficult times is not why the suffering is happening, but what God can do in our situation. Enduring the hardest of times can draw us nearer to God, and we later walk away from the situation knowing God more personally, as Job did. Of his experience, Job said, "I have heard of thee by the hearing of the ear: but now my eye seeth thee" (Job 42:5 KJV). No longer was Job just hearing about God and basing his faith on the word of others, but he was experiencing God's presence in a new and personal way.

God desires this same intimate relationship with each believer, for He desires to draw nearer to each of us. Our lives should reflect total commitment to Jesus, renunciation of worldly ways, and complete obedience to God's will with the desire to further the kingdom of God. Despite the cost, and even when we don't understand the suffering, our desire should be to serve Him, for God works all things together for good.

Suffering will come to true believers.
But suffering benefits the building of our character.
And it establishes an intimate relationship with the Lord.
God desires that we grow spiritually
as we prepare for life in His holy kingdom for all eternity.
Suffering is temporary; godliness is permanent.
In heaven there will be no more mourning or pain.
Suffering now for Christ is a privilege.

―⁂―

The loss of my husband the following month after I had brain surgery opened my eyes over the next couple of years to the two sides of suffering. The physical and emotional pain had overshadowed my life, and it took time for me to refocus and see what God was doing in my circumstances, as He walked me through the valley of Baca.

Some dear Christian friends deserted me, but others came forward and proved to be faithful people whom I could count on. The real turning point came months later as God directed my life into a completely new channel. I had been in despair that there was little hope for my future, until I took the focus off of me personally and started studying about the attributes of God. Deep physical and emotional pain had held me in its grip until I began again to focus on God's character alone. What happened is hard to explain, but gradually the negative hold began to loosen, and a step at a time, I gained new ground.

I became active in the south Snohomish County grief group for the widowed. Despite my physical appearance, I felt loved by those who had an understanding of some of the pain that I was going through. God first directed me into facilitating grief sessions, and then He opened the door for me to do all sorts of counseling from premarital to crisis counseling. God used my pain to cement my relationship with Him. He provided new relationships, new means of survival, new job responsibilities, and new opportunities to enjoy life with my daughter and new friends. God also used my suffering to get people to listen to what I was sharing. Somehow knowing I had endured great personal pain got their attention. For me, a whole new page of life started to unfold, as I gradually got back up on my feet after months of agony. I saw the blessings the Lord poured out as I entered the valley of Berachah.

God was proving His faithfulness and dependability to me during those hard days. He put me on a completely different path than I had pictured I would walk during this particular season of life. This forced me to grow into the potential that He had placed in me at my conception. All the pain, agony, and physical loss were balanced by the changes in my life brought about by God.

Suffering can force us to refocus and make some changes. The uncomfortable pain can draw us closer to God and help us see what more we are capable of accomplishing and becoming. Suffering helped me really lean on God and know how true He can be.

There are two sides of suffering! The actual pain can drive us to the point of brokenness and despair, leaving us with no hope of relief. Yet at that point we can give up or learn to lean on God. If we choose the latter, then God can work to reveal our deeper potential and mold us into transformed people. Pain and suffering can serve a good purpose that will have an eternal effect in our lives. Life is not the same once God is allowed to stretch us to a new level of spiritual growth. What can God do with our suffering? Much more than we know!

Review:

God has a claim on our life both as Creator and Redeemer. Therefore, suffering can produce spiritual growth in us, if we turn to God. Whatever befalls us and causes us pain, can benefit the spreading of the gospel, when we stand for Christ. Our brokenness also can bring about our relying on God and allowing Him to shape our character.

Closing Remarks:

Suffering comes to all believers in some form.
God promises to not allow more than we can bear.
Turning to God benefits our life.
Enduring hard times helps us see the faithfulness of God.
Experiencing God's presence helps us know Him personally.

Chapter Eight

THE INTENDED ABUNDANT LIFE

Abundant life is an offer from Christ of a richer and fuller life now and throughout eternity. God desires that we will experience abundant blessings when we live for Him. The key to such a life though remains a secret to many, and to some extent even to those who believe in the Lord. What Christ offers is in contrast to worldly living. To be fulfilled, the abundant life demands a close relationship with Him.

> "The thief comes only to steal and kill and destroy;
> I came that they may have life,
> and have it abundantly."
> (John 10:10)

Q: How do we as Christians live the abundant and conquering life?

A: Jesus not only offers salvation to the lost, but also an abundant life to those who follow Him (John 10:10). As Christians, we need not settle for less. As the Good Shepherd, Jesus offers a close personal relationship to each member of His flock. He began by extending a way back to God to those who believe in Him, for He paid the price for our sins on Calvary (John 10:11). But, the Lord also desires to shower our lives with blessings as we live for Him (Ezekiel 34:23). As the Good Shepherd, He offers leadership, constant companionship, daily guidance, marvelous peace, contentment, security, and unfailing care to those who trust Him. Our desire should be to obtain what He so freely offers.

Jesus further declared, "I am the way, and the truth, and the life; no one comes to the Father but through Me" (John 14:6). His Word indicates not only what He did on Calvary that we might have eternal life, but what He is doing *now*. The Lord stands in heaven ready to assist in our daily needs as the mediator between God and man (1 Timothy 2:5). That is an awesome position with tremendous possibilities! Jesus takes an active part in each request or supplication we, as Christians, make in prayer to God. Maybe He simply reminds God that this prayer is coming from one of their own.

Jesus also discloses Himself more to those who love Him and keep God's commandments (John 14:21). Thus, as we submit to God's will and do what God has established for our good, Christians are drawn closer to both the Lord Jesus and the Father. The Helper, "the Spirit of Truth" the Lord promised each believer, becomes an active part in moving our life toward fulfillment and the overflowing abundance of God's grace (John 14:16). Jesus said that this Spirit was His Spirit, and He would indwell each believer. This is a very personal matter to the Lord. In various ways, the Lord makes His presence clear to us as our life events unfold.

The Scriptures further express the impossibility for us, who believe, to be separated from the love of Christ Jesus. We

Christians are more than conquerors in spiritual warfare, when we rely on Him (Romans 8:26-39). All this shows His desire for us to experience the abundant life. The battle belongs to the Lord and we are really learning spectators. It is best that we remember that!

Victory comes to those who realize the reality of the fullness of the Lord's indwelling presence by the Holy Spirit in each person who loves Him. When we keep our eyes off our own weaknesses, insufficiency, worthless feelings, foolish pride, etc., and simply follow Him, then we can *overcome* by His grace. This promise of abundant life does not imply that Christians will not face suffering, but it is a guarantee that we will have sufficient means from God to go through whatever comes along. Also, we are assured that He walks through these battles with us.

When we recognize the promises offered in God's Word, and claim them in our Christian walk, we will have *hope, expectations, and assurance* that we can count on God, knowing that He will do something to benefit our struggles. Living a life of holiness brings more strength and power to those in need. Our lifestyle declares who we are in Christ Jesus as sons and daughters of God (Galatians 4:5-6).

How do we live the abundant life and conquer the situations that attempt to overcome us? The Lord Jesus declared that apart from Him we can do nothing (John 15:5). While we cannot do anything on our own, neither are we left alone to handle life. He is our source of *strength* and *power*. If we remain close to Him, we can succeed. All we need to do is ask Christ to help us in our daily walk. When we do, the Lord is pleading our cause in heaven, extending out to us what is best. We can enjoy life through His power. So let us strive to become one with Christ Jesus.

God extends blessings to those who faithfully follow Him. He loves to bless all that we put our hand to in life (Deuteronomy 28:8). When we diligently obey God, His storehouse in heaven will open as a reward for our love.

> The abundant life is what God desires for believers.
> He has more than enough grace to see us through all of life.
> This grace is available when we ask for help.
> The indwelling Spirit will guide our thoughts and actions.
> A Christian is never alone!
> All we need do is trust our God to sustain us and bless our days.
> Abundant life is part of God's gift of salvation
> when we daily turn to Him.

While I've never lived in an elaborate or fancy decorated house, I've always had adequate shelter in a clean, middle-class home. I recall when I was only five that my father bought a lovely, brand-new living room sofa and chair. Shortly afterward, my folks divorced and all the new furniture was gone. For a while we lived with my oldest sister in a hut during World War II, but it was still a warm place that we called home.

Even in the poorest of times, there was always food in the cupboard, clothes to wear during the hot summers and cold winters, and a place of shelter that was our mailing address. We had no electricity or phones during my early years, but I rode bikes or horses with my friends and we swam in rivers near my home.

My generation of friends didn't think of fancy cars, ballroom dances, or nights out on the town. Years later at our fiftieth high school graduation anniversary, one of the guys said, "We were dirt poor, and didn't know it." How true! But we never felt neglected or wanting, for we all shared something this present generation can't seem to find—peace and contentment in our state of affairs.

An abundant life doesn't consist necessarily of a lot of material things, although those are not ruled out. An abundant life has more spirituality in it than it contains material possessions. The quality of life based on a relationship with God shines through. My classmates and I were privileged to enjoy the relationships we shared with each other and with God. Peace, love, joy, and contentment are all hard to find among inanimate possessions, but those qualities were part of our lives, as most of our generation knew God. We truly had an abundant life based on love. God has always provided me with more than enough of His "treasures," not gold and silver, but His faithfulness.

Review:
An abundant life is available for both now and throughout eternity. Settling for less keeps us from experiencing a close walk with the Lord. God wants to freely bless our lives. As our mediator, Christ Jesus extends our prayers to God for answers. How our life unfolds is a very personal matter to the Lord Jesus.

Closing Remarks:
Christians are more than conquerors in spiritual warfare.
Nothing can separate us from the love of God.
God will provide the means to overcome whatever is necessary.
He desires that we experience the abundant life.
Living a life of holiness is done by His power and strength.
An abundant life consists of real contentment where we are.

Chapter Nine

TOP PRIORITIES

Priorities are essential in our life, for there are certain important issues and considerations that should come first. The values we cherish determine in what order we handle things. Our behavior, speech, actions, and deeds reflect what we consider as being the most important. Being a Christian should shape our thinking and behavior so that our life pleases God. His desire is to pour out blessings on those whose lives show a good example by how they live.

> They profess to know God, but by their deeds they deny Him,
> being detestable and disobedient and
> worthless for any good deed.
> (Titus 1:16)

Q: What should the Christian hold as top priorities in his or her life?

A: Viewing life as a Christian is like viewing the valley below from a mountaintop that allows us to see and obtain a greater perspective on things. While hiking, the higher we climb, the greater our view, until before us spreads a grand sight of wonder, often striking our minds with a sense of disbelief. So it is in our spiritual walk with God. Getting to the top, or maturing, is important and offers a greater perspective on all of life. As we climb upward spiritually, each step enlarges the scene before us. The more we mature as Christians, the more our spiritual growth affects who we are, what we think, how we behave, and our perspective on things.

During the early steps of our spiritual walk through life, we "climb" a low rolling knoll and catch just a glimpse of God. Later, we extend our walk to the top of an insignificant problem "hill," and we begin to get a glimmer of how much our God has to offer. Once we move on and conquer the majestic whole "mountain," we find a glorious view spread before us. All around is the faithfulness and love of the One who cares for our very soul and every step that we take. Each step of our climb results in discovering more of the beautiful blessings that God has to offer His people. Our perspective on things changes, our view of others and events enlarges, and our spiritual growth in life expands as we climb, because God becomes the center of our focus.

Life's journey doesn't end with our conquering that first "mountain" of life and learning what is there. Each step we take means we are growing and fulfilling our place in the world. Advancing simply opens the doors of opportunity for us to proclaim our Lord more to those who need Him. Isaiah, the Old Testament prophet, said, "Go up on a high mountain" and proclaim the good news of God (Isaiah 40:9 NIV). Thus, as Christians, some things should become constant priorities in our lives. Here are a few suggestions:

- Our first priority must be a total commitment to God. Loyalty to Him reflects the love we have for our Creator. This is simply acknowledging our personal attachment to the One who gives us life, love, guidance, and meaning (Matthew 22:37). Nothing should come before this priority. A glance at our lifestyle should show our love for God, our maker.
- Our second priority should be to love our neighbor as ourselves. Getting to know who we are and learning to realize our own worth is the foundation for all other relationships. We are instructed by the Lord Jesus to love others, as we love our self (Matthew 22:39). Reaching out to people, and offering a portion of the love we have so generously been given by God, should be our goal (1 Thessalonians 3:12). This priority should start with our family and then go on beyond to our neighbors and other acquaintances.
- Our third priority should be pleasing God by knowing and doing His will (Ephesians 6:6). When we learn God has given us all our talents, abilities, and gifts then we can function best in handling life and living up to His plan for us. We are called to be a part of God's kingdom, and we need to learn how to walk worthily of this calling by bearing good fruit (Ephesians 4:1; Colossians 1:10). This begins by studying His Word until it becomes a part of us, keeping in mind that God knows what is best for us.
- Our fourth priority must reflect our being good spiritual examples to others (Philippians 3:17; 1 Corinthians 4:16; 11:1). Offering spiritual leadership to our family, friends, and associates should result in edifying those in need. We all need mentoring and models to follow.

- This is connected to our fifth priority: always trusting and obeying God, our Father. Without questioning, doubting, or wondering, we need to walk in *faith* in all circumstances (Hebrews 11:6). Believing God cares and will help us with life's situations is our base. Not always is this easy to do, but trusting God is very profitable and is our security.
- Our sixth priority should be to allow the Holy Spirit to constantly teach us more of God's holy ways in which to walk (John 14:26). This stretches our spiritual muscles and strengthens our outreach to others. Heeding the Spirit's teaching keeps us on the positive path of life, helps us avoid negative things, and enhances our working relationship with the Spirit, who also prepares Christians to be ready for the next assignment of life that God may choose to give us.
- Another outstanding priority is to be ready for the Lord's second coming. This seventh area of our lives should not be taken lightly, for the Lord Jesus Himself emphasized the importance of preparation for this great event (John 14:3; Matthew 16:27, 24:31, 44). Because the exact time of His return is unknown, being ready daily is essential! Christ's return will make our decision final. There will be no second chance to change or prepare.
- A final priority to be shared springs from the above, knowing the Lord will soon come. A realization that there are those who are lost and need the Great Physician to heal them should become foremost in our minds, when we truly believe in His return. Seeking and helping save the lost by witnessing for Jesus should be

our natural desire as God's love flows to and through us. Once Christians climb the "mountain" of life, mature in the process and see things from God's perspective, our purpose becomes imperative to share the wonders of God, reach out to the lost, and to do it all for God's glory (2 Peter 3:9, Matthew 28:18-20).

While there are other priorities that are important in one's life, these mentioned above should give a person a good foundation to work from during their earthly journey.

Enjoy your holy walk daily with the Lord and your climb to a higher view of life by setting these priorities as your own fixed obligation to God and yourself. Growing in the Lord becomes easier with a broader view of life from God's perspective. Seek to do things His way and reap the best results.

> Being holy should be our top priority.
> Letting our life shine for Christ is part of
> who we are in the Lord.
> The things that are important to us speak loudly
> of our loyalty or disloyalty to Him.
> Don't be deceived or try to deceive God.
> Our thoughts, actions, and words speak volumes.
> God already knows our lifestyles.

In the early years of my marriage, I occasionally worked part-time as an assistant cook for the Bible college, or I volunteered in the office as a bookkeeper, or in the library as a helper sorting books. I enjoyed assisting wherever I was needed, when I had free time. While I loved being part of college life even briefly, these tasks were not top priorities to me. I didn't desire a career outside of my home. Being a wife and a mother was a full-time job. Things related to that job were my priorities.

One of the best relationships available to anyone is a lasting marriage relationship that literally joins a man and a woman together. If the marriage is begun on an unselfish basis, then the relationship will grow and deepen. But to ensure this will happen, both parties must enter the marriage with total commitment. The importance of placing the needs of one's spouse and the family first as an essential priority brings success. Unselfish relationships are the most successful.

My husband and I thought alike. Held the same interests. Sought to live by the same values. And, our family and friends came first after our relationship with God. Expanding our education and remaining healthy were considered essential by both of us, so we pursued degrees to gain more biblical knowledge and enjoyed recreational times together. Our priorities became keeping our perspective in line with God's, and being faithful stewards of what He entrusted to our care. We had harmony in our relationship, even though we were both growing and changing during our years together. The things we gave preference to helped us maintain order in our busy lives. By not allowing other people or events to override our priorities, we enjoyed a good life together and influenced our children to do the same.

Review:

Certain things have to come first in life. How we live reflects what we consider our top priorities. Discovering more of the faithfulness and awesome love of God expands our view of life. Our perspective on people and things will change for the better, and we will begin to fulfill our purpose for being alive, when we look at life from God's perspective.

Closing Remarks:
Loyalty to God should be first.
Loving others comes with loving who we are.
Walking worthily of our calling comes with doing God's will.
Being good spiritual examples edifies others.
Walking in faith comes from trusting God.
We need to heed the Spirit's teaching and promptings.
Be ready for the second coming of Christ Jesus.
Witnessing for Christ shows our love for Him and others.

Chapter Ten

COMPOSURE IN DIFFICULTIES

Keeping one's feelings under control has become obsolete to a large degree in our society. People continue to put themselves before others and strike out in harmful ways. Lack of self control brings more destruction to themselves and innocent others nearby. While remaining composed in difficult situations takes lots of effort, self-control and calmness spare us from harmful consequences in the end.

> Stop depriving one another . . .
> Come together again so that Satan will not tempt you
> because of your lack of self-control.
> (1 Corinthians 7:5)

Q: How do Christians remain composed in the difficult times of life?

A: A whirling storm that spins off destructive power in a few seconds can level whatever is in its path. The furious winds of tornadoes rip up complete communities, leaving behind un-repairable damage to life and property in the wake of its destruction. What was standing solid and firm one minute before is quickly demolished by the explosive forces let loose. Families in the path of such storms can be torn apart, lives lost, and ever so many lives permanently changed.

One's life, it's true, can be like a treacherous hurricane or a twisting tornado without self-control. Some people today allow their lives to be used in similar destructive ways. Loved ones are crushed by their outlandish behavior. Physical harm is done hastily to the family, and even close friends. While energy is used up unproductively, death or damage can result because of anger and lack of thought. Assets are foolishly lost by bad decisions, gambling, or pure wastefulness. Picture in your mind the permanent destruction done once the fury begins. Even words spoken cannot be retraced.

In nature when a storm occurs, the center of a hurricane has a calm area called the eye, where little wind movement actually happens. That center has a stillness and tranquility that is much like the peacefulness and righteousness of God in a Christian's life who is living for Christ (2 Corinthians 13:11). No matter how furious life's troubles may be, as a follower of Christ Jesus, His peace becomes the subduing force that offers confidence, rest, and an abundance of serenity for those who rely on Him. As life all around reflects the twisted worldly way of bitterness, frustration, violence, and hatred, a Christian can remain composed, because the Holy Spirit dwells within him or her and brings self-control (Jeremiah 33:5-6; Galatians 5:22-23).

For the believing Christian, God offers both physical and emotional protection and security. The human spirit can remain tranquil by the inner strength and grace that comes from God, not from our own ability. Under His outstretched "wings" there is freedom from anxiety, doubt, fear, and exposure to real danger (Philippians 4:7). God guards His own people. When Christians find themselves under attack, and the "storms" of life seem overwhelming, then they must look for the calmness of the "eye" that God offers. His serenity is available to those who turn to Him. By determination and faith, a Christian can move on in God's power. In His hands, we find safety and protection, for our God reigns (Psalm 91).

We, as Christians, do not have to let our feelings control us. Too often, we tend to allow feelings to reign. Although our feelings are God-given, how we respond to them is our responsibility. The Holy Spirit offers us patience and self-control to help regulate our lives—two necessary ingredients for a composed life. We need to determine within ourselves how we will react in any given situation. Will we accept the Spirit's help to control our responses? By asking for help to restrain our emotions, we can respond beautifully in the worst of conditions, not just react without thought. Without the help of the Spirit, we will fail. Learning to discipline ourselves prevents greater disasters from affecting our lives. Restrain can benefit us personally when we remain within certain desired boundary lines established by God. Composure in trying times may be difficult, but not impossible with the help of God.

Self-control is a fruit of the Holy Spirit.
Lack of self-control is something Satan uses to destroy people.
Keeping our feelings under control speaks
volumes as to who we are.
Composure in hard situations is a beautiful thing,
and it reaps much for our benefit.

As a counselor, I have seen people struggle and lose control in sessions, yet I had to maintain my composure, if I hoped to bring about peace and progress in their relationships. Often the client just needed a place to vent his or her feelings and regain self-control. People can only do this if others show them empathy and remain calm.

Sadly, I've seen Christians also become upset with their brothers and sisters in the Lord over some simple misunderstandings. They forgot what real love is all about—genuine, sincere concern and affection—and they tend to lash out with their feelings as they lose self-control. Composure is often the last thing they are thinking about, for they are centered on their problems.

We are all becoming more and more aware of the road rage, domestic disputes, and senseless shootings in malls or schools that are being revealed on evening newscasts. Anger now has more daily control in our society than self-control. There is a real need to show love for others, regain self-control, and not express rage. We overcome evil by doing good.

Sometimes in life we find ourselves in trying and testing situations. People can easily misunderstand in those hard moments who we are or what we have said or done. Other times they may have expectations that we don't fulfill, and those disappointments can tear apart relationships. Without composure, it is hard to work through such misunderstandings.

Composure shows our state of maturity, while the lack of self-control can reflect the stress we are under and our need for extra help. We are instructed in the Word of God to take every thought captive, or under control, for the Lord. This means we are to hold each word with such force that we overcome that negative feeling and not act on it in a destructive way. The Holy Bible even says to not let the sun set on our anger, because those uncontrolled feelings allow the devil to have access to our lives. Thus, we become in peril with that door wide open. Becoming upset over certain matters is not wrong, but what we do with our feelings is our responsibility.

Composure only becomes easy if we allow the Holy Spirit to function in our life. The Bible says to not quench the Spirit! Putting out His power in our lives means we have to struggle alone, and that is not God's intended way for He wants to assist His children.

Review:

Self-control is critical to avoid harmful consequences that can permanently affect all of our lives. Destruction and an unchangeable outcome can result from lack of thought and self-restrain. How we respond in any situation is our responsibility. Self-discipline is the key, and our strength and peace will come from God, if we ask.

Closing Remarks:

Do not open the door for the devil to destroy your life.
Control and express all your feelings in a positive way.
Quench not the Holy Spirit.
Allow the Spirit of God to inspire your responses.

Chapter Eleven

OVERCOMING NEGATIVE THOUGHTS

God has given us the ability to reason things out in our mind, and He offers to help us do so. Choosing to not let negative thoughts control us is within our ability. The choice is ours! Negative thinking spirals downward the more we give in to such thoughts, escalating rapidly to our own destruction when not controlled. The Scriptures encourage us to seek the pure things of life and concentrate on what is beautiful and profitable.

> We are destroying speculations and every lofty thing
> raised up against the knowledge of God, and
> we are taking every thought captive to the obedience of Christ.
> (2 Corinthians 10:5)

Q: Many times our minds are flooded with negative thoughts. What should we do to control our thinking and restore our peace of mind?

A: Negative thoughts result in destructive actions, if allowed to remain in control. Such thoughts even produce conflict within us, causing health issues. When the mind becomes in a disturbed state; fear, doubt, envy, anxiety, jealousy, selfishness, discouragement, despair, loss of hope, and the act of giving up can affect our lives. When anger or discouragement controls our thinking, those thoughts leave the door open for the devil to plant more negative thoughts and bring about destructive actions. This is something the devil likes to do for he comes to steal, to kill, and to destroy (John 10:10). He is our enemy and may attempt to plant the wrong spirit(s) in us.

Solomon declared in Proverbs 23:7 that a person acts according to how he or she thinks. Our thinking affects our progress in life or lack of it. We act based on what we concentrate on. But, Solomon also says one should "Apply your heart to discipline and your ears to words of knowledge" (Proverbs 23:12). That is wise counsel! Here God offers the solution: self-discipline and more understanding of His Word, for real wisdom comes from above. Whatever information we put into our minds will guide our thoughts and actions, be it for good or bad results.

Peter, who was impetuous before Christ's resurrection, often spoke without serious thought. But he became a very different man after he knew the risen Jesus as his Lord and Savior. Peter later instructed Christians to "gird your minds for action" (1 Peter 1:13). As believers, we must equip our minds with God's truth to prepare the best we can for any encounters. Peter further stated that believers should be "obedient children" and "holy in all their behavior" (vs. 14-15).

As followers of Christ, we can only do that if we take control of our thoughts. Christians must base their philosophy of life on God's principles. If believers hold to God's standard, there will be no place for worry and anxiety in their lives. Trusting God is the key. Learning His Word gives wisdom.

The apostle Paul emphatically said he would destroy every speculation that opposed God's Word, and take "every thought captive to the obedience of Christ" (2 Corinthians 10:5). The key word is obedience. Out of reverence to the Lord, and what He has done for us, we should be motivated to obey. King Solomon had also declared this same principle when he said, "live in the fear of the Lord always" (Proverbs 23:17). The fear he is referring to is reverence; a deep respect for God should control our lives.

Paul enhanced the solution that Solomon wrote about in his letter to the Philippians. While he wrote from prison, Paul never let his experiences make him become negative, sour on life, or embittered. He simply kept his focus on Christ Jesus, whom he loved and trusted. In the darkest days of suffering, and there were many, Paul's faith was tested and proven genuine because of how he responded. The peace of God, which "surpasses all comprehension," was what guarded Paul's life (Philippians 4:7).

Paul expands our knowledge by saying to pray when you are anxious. If we are to be one with God, then we must accept His offer of help to reason things out. We do that by requesting His help through our prayers (Isaiah 1:18). Inviting God to be a part of the difficulties that concern us is the beginning step. Then Paul declared the next step is to remove the negative and worldly thoughts by dwelling on the beautiful and joyful things of life. The apostle is instructing Christians to nurture the pure things, not the negative things of life. To cherish and cultivate the finer things keeps us positive. We will establish a good and confident thought pattern by not allowing the negative to govern our actions. Think instead on the pure, the true, the honorable, the right, the good, and the lovely things worthy of praise. That is God's advice.

Christ said, "Love the Lord your God with all your heart, and with all your soul, and with all your mind, and with all your strength" (Mark 12:30). When we love God, we will be focused on the positive. We know from looking at nature that God, as Creator, loves beautiful things. So whatever form of beauty that crosses our path is what we should be concentrating on. Man has the God-given ability to reason; we can control our thought patterns by inviting God to help us see what is best. When we do our part, the peace of God will flood and guard our hearts and minds.

> Negative thoughts can keep one from his potential.
> Our focus should remain on the One who
> holds the answers—God.
> The Word of God offers solutions to our problems.
> Study God's Word to be prepared for whatever comes.
> Concentrate on the lovely things and dispel the negative thoughts.
> Inner peace then will be our blessing from God.

As a retired counselor, I recall many clients who expressed only negative thoughts as they shared their feelings and situations. No matter what had happened in their lives, all they could see was the negative side of the circumstances. Yet, regardless of what is occurring, there can be both good, as well as bad, found in the events. Some situations point out changes we need to make in our lives that can be helpful. We need to recognize these areas before we can act positively on them.

"What might have been," is a touching expression of disappointment, when reality comes knocking at our door. The statement conveys that things could have been different. Often we miss the mark and fail to live up to our full potential, mostly because we allowed negative thoughts to creep in and control our life. We may have climbed higher mountains had we tried. We could have accomplished more had we used all of our talents to the fullest. We could have enjoyed the brighter side of life, if we had concentrated more on the good in every situation. Things could have turned out differently had we chosen to focus only on the good.

To be successful, working with clients in counseling sessions meant those negative thoughts had to be exchanged for more positive thinking. Their thoughts had to include both the positive and the negative, and they had to consider all the alternative actions that were available. God instructs us to "Set your mind on the things above" (Colossians 3:2), because He knows how distracting and discouraging worldly things can be. But, looking at the positive rather than just the negative, gives more possibilities to consider. Being positive reflects our character—the essential qualities or attributes within that conveys life from God's perspective—and others come to know who we really are.

Review:

Negative thoughts spiral downward and escalate in our personal destruction. The real solution is expanding our knowledge of God, which restores our peace of mind. Our actions, be they good or bad, are the outcome of our thinking. God expects us to be holy, showing love.

Closing Remarks:

True wisdom is from above.
Learning more of God's standard offers real guidance.
Deep reverence for God motivates Christians to obey.
God's peace becomes our peace where positive thoughts reign.
Cherish and cultivate the finer things of life.

Chapter Twelve

IMPORTANT ENCOUNTERS

Our communication with God by prayer brings more knowledge of God's way of doing things. When we enter God's throne room and are in His presence we will be personally changed. When we approach our Holy God, we realize how fortunate we are to have the privilege to be with Him. Knowing the holiness of the Creator of the universe drives home in our thoughts how small and insignificant humans can be on their own.

> Therefore let us therefore draw near with confidence
> to the throne of grace, so that we may receive mercy
> and find grace to help in time of need.
> (Hebrews 4:16)

Q: What really happens when we come into God's presence in prayer?

A: When Christians come to God in prayer, we have the privilege of being in His very presence. We will walk away changed from our encounter. We are touched by His power and strength, and reassured of His will in *all* matters. Time spent in prayer affirms that God is in control, even if we must wait for answers.

In Hebrews 4:16, the author declares that believers can "draw near in confidence." Have you ever completely comprehended what is being offered to Christians in this inspired passage of Scripture? We may freely come before God with our requests, asking in Jesus' name, and *receive a hearing* before God, our Creator. Being a Christian gives us access to our heavenly Father, our Holy God Himself. Being in His presence is a very privileged encounter.

In the Old Testament days not many people were allowed in God's presence. In the garden, Adam and Eve were fortunate and allowed to walk with God before sin came in and destroyed their relationship. After their failure to live obediently to God's Word, that privilege was removed. No longer could man, because of sin, walk freely with his Holy God.

Moses, when he was given the Ten Commandments on the mountain and requested to see God, was permitted only a glimpse of God's back. Even the effects of this limited encounter were outstanding. We are told that Moses' face shone with God's glory from being in His presence, so much so, that when he descended again to the Israelite people, they could not withstand the reflection of God on his face. They asked for Moses to be veiled when he returned. Such glory is overwhelming to sinful man.

In a vision years later, Isaiah, the prophet, also saw God's glory. He had been given the rare privilege of seeing God sitting on His throne in heaven and filling the temple with His glory. Isaiah declared, "I saw the Lord sitting on a throne, lofty and exalted, with the train of His robe filling the temple" (Isaiah 6:1). The scene revealed God's greatness, His indescribable majesty, and His awesome power. Then an angel called out, "Holy, Holy, Holy is the Lord of hosts, the whole earth is full of His glory" (Isaiah 6:3). The result of Isaiah seeing God left him in full knowledge of his own sinfulness. What a tremendous vision! What a revealing privilege!

In the New Testament days, when the shepherds heard the proclamation of the good news that the Savior Christ Jesus was born in Bethlehem, "the glory of the Lord shone around them" (Luke 2:9). They were left trembling in fear because of the overwhelming experience. Later in Revelation, the apostle John, while on the island of Patmos, also heard and saw the Son in His glory, as Christ Jesus revealed to him the final words of the Bible. During this revelation, John was taken up into heaven and allowed to see God sitting on His throne, while myriads of angels proclaimed His worthiness to be worshipped.

The matchless splendor of God is overwhelming to those who are given a view of God. But because of what Jesus has done for us on the cross, Christians can now boldly and confidently stand in God's presence and speak to Him through prayer. While not a visible encounter with God, speaking directly to God is an awesome privilege. We no longer stand condemned, filthy from sin, but are saved and redeemed. We do not need to fear being in God's presence. Without Christ standing in as our mediator though, God's splendor and glory would overpower and crush us.

As Moses, Isaiah, the shepherds, the apostle John, and others were deeply touched and changed by their encounters with God, so are we who believe in Jesus and come to God in prayer. Our prayers cease to be empty words, repeatedly murmured because they sound good. Our prayers become real-life communication with our Maker, and we simply grow closer to God each day as we pray and see God faithfully answering our prayers. Life becomes an uplifting and exciting experience, as we begin to comprehend what God *can and will do* for His people, all because we ask Him in prayer. These are privileged times and life-changing encounters.

Others, too, begin to see more clearly the reflection of God placed on those who trust Him, just as the Israelites saw this special reflection on Moses. God's people think more positively. They have a peace beyond understanding inside them. Worldly things no longer burden them down. Believers seem to have new direction and reachable goals. Thus, they strive to use all their potential for God. Christians then become faithful stewards. There is a new ability to love within them. In their eyes, there is compassion, which gives their faces a new, peaceful composure. All this and much more is reflected out from God's people who truly have been in His presence through awesome prayer encounters.

Those who practice reading God's Word, listening to what He says, giving more time to Him, and are in God's presence through prayer are *changed* people. They become *humble* people, who receive God's *grace, comfort, love, peace*, and His *mercy*. They walk in His *power and strength*, because they take time to pray. Christians then become His ambassadors with His saving message for others. They have left their old ways behind and are being transformed by His glory. God's presence changes people, and He does this when we come before Him in prayer!

Praying to God changes who we are.
His holiness proclaims our need for His attributes.
Deep communication with our heavenly Father
will bring about our own needed transformation.
Each day we see His faithfulness reaffirming we can trust Him.
God's grace sustains us, and His mercy exercises His deep
compassion and His forgiveness, as He helps us with life.

Over the years, the one thing that has helped me most to endure life's struggles, pain, and problems has been prayer. Raising a big family meant lots of accidents involving the kids, which needed medical attention. Falls, bike and swing accidents, slingshot mishaps, and attempts at climbing trees, all meant trips to the doctor's office or the hospital. Grief over the loss of loved ones and other events also required much prayer. Three of my children had major head traumas during their growing up years, and each episode was a time of need that required knee-bending prayer.

Some events are overwhelming, and other happenings drain us of all our reserved strength and other difficulties leave us questioning why we even live. Yet these times will either draw us to God or force us to bear the burden in our own power, the best we can. If we attempt to handle the load in our own strength, we are settling for less than what God desires for us. He always wants what is best for us and offers the right resource for each situation, when asked.

I learned early on that God cares about every detail of our lives, and He desires to answer our prayers with His faithful responses. We don't have to be anxious about the problems life throws at us, for the peace of God does guard our hearts when we pray. These times of need result in life-altering encounters with our Creator.

Prayer is more than communicating with a close friend, although God is that, because our requests open the way for God's best resources to become ours. His storehouse in heaven holds whatever will benefit our lives. God strengthens us as we pray, and He supplies all our needs, when we reverently submit our requests to Him and acknowledge His will.

In the hardest of times, when there was little hope, the uplifting strength that came from God and His comforting peace assured me that God heard and answered my prayers. The Almighty is a God of love, and He shows it beautifully when we are at our last straw, broken, and hopeless. The outstanding principle that I learned about prayer is that you don't have to be in the last stage of helplessness before God responds; He loves to be there anytime we come to Him. He is faithful to His Word!

Review:

Humans apart from God are not effective or fruitful. Prayer gives us a hearing before our Creator. Prayer also confirms that God is in control. To have access to God and speak directly to Him is an awesome privilege, and it can be a life-changing encounter! God's way of doing things becomes more familiar to those who pray often.

Closing Remarks:

Prayer is real communication with our Maker.
Believers change from prayer encounters with God.
God's people reflect that they have been in His presence.
God's resources become ours when we approach the Lord.

Chapter Thirteen

RESTING IN JESUS

In this demanding world we all need time to recharge, renew, and recover losses, be they physical or mental. Being exhausted bodily and emotionally means we need a time of privacy and communion with Christ Jesus. Jesus promises to give rest to those who come to Him. He is very aware of our needs. Our Maker personally cares! Making time though is our responsibility.

> And He said to them, "Come away by yourselves
> to a secluded place and rest a while."
> (Mark 6:31)

Q: How can we learn to rest in Jesus when life's circumstances steamroll over us at times, and things are beyond our control?

A: The answer is offered by Jesus in Matthew 11:28-30: "Come to Me, all who are weary and heavy-laden, and I will give you rest. Take My yoke upon you, and learn from Me, for I am gentle and humble in heart, and you will find rest for your souls. For My yoke is easy, and My burden is light." Jesus cares about the spiritual part of our being's needs—soul—and our physical need to also take a break from daily labor. Here the Lord makes a promise to give us renewal, if we come to Him. Moreover, He offers inner peace to the weary. Because He carries the load, our lives become easier and lighter, when we surrender to His care.

Because God cursed the earth when sin came in, due to man's disobedience, labor to produce our livelihood is now hard. We often toil until we become physically exhausted. We also become weary from ministering to others, while extending the kingdom of God. The physical, mental, and spiritual areas of our lives are often affected and we need a break. To remain effective in our labors, be it physical labor or doing God's work reaching out to others spiritually, we need periodic rest.

The three active words in the above Scripture: *come, take,* and *learn,* offer the solution to our need for rest. Jesus, the true Shepherd, is the One who sets the pace for those who surrender to His Lordship. When a Christian submits to His yoke of leadership, that person has stepped within the framework of discipleship that the Lord Himself established. He directs our course, and part of His leadership role is to recognize our need for rest. Coming to Jesus includes allowing Him to carry the load, so that we can have time for a retreat. Just going to a simple place for some quiet time can lift our spirit and body, as we encounter the Lord's strength and nearness.

A yoke is simply a device and symbol of subjection that binds or connects us closely side by side with the Lord. When we become Christians and are united in a new relationship with Him, we are joined together as a team to get the job done. When we take up the yoke of service, we are remaining within the guidelines offered by Christ for He called us to serve.

Learning from the Lord begins with understanding God is in control of all things. When we feel overwhelmed and overloaded by the demands, God, the Father, will use such distressing times to help us trust Him more. Christians can be reassured that if God permits inexplicable and painful experiences to come into our days, His hand is still at work in our circumstances. While invisible to us, God is very active. He is the source of all we require and is there in the middle of situations whether they are trying or fun events. Our own self-reliance needs to be laid aside, so we can learn to depend more and more on Him. The darkest of times can be used by the Lord to fulfill His will in our lives (Matthew 27:45, Job 1, 2).

Limitations, difficulties, and distressing seasons are learning times for all of God's children, just as much as the good days. Such times reveal that we have immediate access to the full privileges of being children of God (Romans 8:15-16). During hard times, we can learn to allow the Holy Spirit, our Comforter, to help us as He intercedes during our prayers (Romans 8:26, Acts 9:31). Such times become precious moments of learning that "God causes all things to work together for good" (Romans 8:28). Beyond those difficult times lies the realization that God is in the process of conforming us to the very image of His Son (Romans 8:29). Blessings, gifts, and special benefits come in unexpected moments, showing God's faithfulness as He "freely gives us all things" necessary to handle life (Romans 8:32).

Let us not forget that the Lord Jesus Himself is at "the right hand of God" interceding for us too (Romans 8:34). Beyond all the possible disturbing experiences we go through, Christians can overcome, survive, and even conquer through Him who loves us (Romans 8:37).

Stepping apart for a period of rest is an important part of our survival. Looking at Elijah's life, we can see how God ministered to him by sending His angels when Elijah was weary. God's power, strength and grace will carry us through whatever we are asked to endure, and He freely offers these when we retreat for rest. We can rest in Jesus, since we are never alone.

So when we come to the Lord, take up His yoke, and learn from Christ Jesus, rest too will come from the day-by-day tests and trials, if we allow Him to be part of the team. Jesus has promised His interception, which can be a part of our daily walk with Him. As a reminder to us, He proclaims that He is a "gentle and humble" leader, willing to restore our weary spirits. Again hear His words as a remembrance, "My yoke is easy, and My burden is light" (Matthew 11:30).

> The task may seem impossible at times.
> Yet, God holds the resources we need.
> To remain effective in our efforts,
> we need to stay close to the Lord and claim a time of rest.
> In His outstretched hand there is support.
> Periodic rest is OK!

One thing we all need is a good night's rest, and a big break from the demands of life. I've gone to several women's retreats and conferences over the years and have walked away with a renewed spirit. Something about the messages and the songs seemed to lift me spiritually. Being alone away from all the demanding activities brought me closer to God, and simultaneously restored the physical needs of my body.

The best retreats are held in places near the ocean, or a quiet lake, or in a green mountain setting, for they seem to bring that inner peace that our bodies need and our souls long for. Those surroundings bring us closer to God just by their stillness and lack of distractions. But those environments allow God to draw closer to us also. Truly, God renews our strength when we spend extra, quiet time with Him.

I've also been in many of the Southwestern mission courtyards and gardens and enjoyed the serene setting and elaborate well-kept lawns. The beautiful flowers abundantly blooming in their beds show the loveliness of nature and life around us.

Many of the national parks across America can also provide a peaceful setting in which one can be alone with our Creator, who desires that we enjoy life.

Often we allow exhaustion to become our enemy. We push as if the world turns on what we do. Yet, doctors will quickly say that our real health problems have to do with our bodies being overworked and physically weary. We need to heed what God has recorded in His Word that we should keep the seventh day of the week open for rest.

If I can't possibly attend a complete retreat, just taking a day off gives me that extra pause that refreshes my soul. But, a whole week at the ocean restores me physically, mentally, and spiritually.

Review:

Physical rest is needed by everyone to restore our strength and energy levels. God cared enough to command that we take a day of rest each week. Surrendering our lives to Christ allows Him to lighten our load, and it makes things flow well.

Closing Remarks:

Life's demands often exhaust us.
God is actively behind the scenes for us to rely on.
Lay aside self-reliance; learn to depend on the Lord.
Periodic rest is an important part of our healthy survival.

Chapter Fourteen

NEVER COMPROMISE THE TRUTH

The blending of two concepts doesn't make it right. Even acknowledging or conceding to an idea doesn't make it so. Our true character and what we believe is reflected in our lifestyle and relationships. We live out God's Word or we fail to comply with His standards by compromising. God's truth is the perfect standard for life. Our society needs His absolute truth for guidance.

> "If you continue in My word, then you are truly disciples
> of Mine; and you will know the truth
> and the truth will make you free."
> (John 8:31-32)

Q: What happens when we compromise on issues that oppose God's Word?

A: Why did Jesus instruct His followers to "not be like the hypocrites" (Matthew 6:16)? What they taught was not in agreement with God's Word. The religious leaders' showy traditions, rituals, and doctrines were simply an empty display of religion. They were meaningless and worthless attempts to worship without a real relationship with God.

Today, the moral and spiritual decline across our nation is reflected in those who favor the use of drugs, abortion, sex without marriage, assisted suicide, gambling, and open displays of violence. Abuse in various forms and random violence against others all indicate a lack of feeling and love that reveals how far man has fallen from what God intended humans to be. Claiming to be a Christian without even attending church is an excuse often used, that also reflects the corruption and sin in a person's life. In our society, we are experiencing more and more indifference among those who are willing to compromise the truth.

Beliefs that oppose God's Word tend literally to drain people of their God-given strength, power, and peace. Every time we veer from the truth, we must face the consequences our change in course brings. As good stewards of God's Word, Christians must remain unwavering by standing firmly for the principles and standards set forth in His revealed Word (Titus 1:9). Sometimes we have to hold fast to the narrow view on important issues, even if it means we are not liked and may be completely rejected. *Knowing the truth is not enough. We must remain faithful to it.*

We have been called by God to walk the Christian walk, and live the Christian faith, not just talk about it (Ephesians 4:1, 5:2; Galatians 5:25; Titus 2:12). That means we must live by God's standards. Those concepts that seem insignificant to us personally can have a profound effect on those around us. We truly influence others by our actions and words, or the lack of conviction and actions that support God's Word. Standing for

God upon His principles and for His standards, is our way of reflecting our thanks to God for all He has done.

As Christians, standing for our convictions based on God's Word becomes a part of our true nature as "born again" believers. Even Jesus declared that the thoughts He presented in His teachings were not His own but came from God, which notes the importance of the source of Jesus' words. He spoke with authority from God. The more Scripture we learn, the more we will understand what God is teaching in various passages of His Word, the stronger our faith becomes, and the more mature we will be in comprehending God's will for our life.

God established His laws, statues, commandments, promises, and ways for our *good* (Deuteronomy 10:12-13). None of His words are just rules to force compliance. They are intended to keep us healthy and strong. Our Holy God desires to show us the way of holiness (Isaiah 35:8-10). He knows what is best for us and has conveyed His standards to help us gain unsurpassed knowledge about life—what really works for our benefit!

Instead of following worldly ways as Christians, let us show our gratitude to the Lord for providing "the way, the truth and the life" through His Son, Jesus (John 14:6), so we may freely have a right relationship with Almighty God. *Today is the day that we as Christians must stand for God's truth.* In His love and with gentle patience, we need to reflect the compassion of Christ to our struggling world. We do that by living as God shows us in Scriptures.

> Compromising often comes easily.
> None of us wants to be rejected or unloved.
> Not holding to the whole truth and surrendering even
> a part of it leads to more false teaching.

> Compromising doesn't make an idea right,
> for God's Word is unchangeable.
> Stand for God's truth by God's power!
> By doing so, we will be establishing great treasures in heaven.
> The greatest treasure will be our relationship with God.

None of us is perfect, but we can learn to walk closer to God's standard each day, as we mature in the knowledge God has given us in the Scriptures. Like a child first learns to crawl, then later with faltering steps learns to walk, or as a little one begins by drinking only milk before solid foods, the individual has to learn spiritual truths in steps.

When working with various clients over the years, I had to determine at what level of spiritual knowledge they were; then my task was to help expand their knowledge to a higher level. People live by what they know through education and experience. Like sponges we drink in knowledge, whether good or bad. Thus, this is why we need a standard of absolute truth and need to rely on it to be able to discern error.

Parents need to be wise in God's Word so that they can share this with their children. This is one of the great instructions of God, when He first started to reveal His laws and commandments to the Israelites. Both morning and evening and all during the day, they were to be teachers of God's truths to their loved ones. He didn't want the children to forget how important was their relationship to Him. That is still true for us today. How much I wished I had known more of God's Word when I was raising my family. But, really learning His absolute truth is a life-long process.

What joy it brings when I see someone who has been stumbling along grasp a truth that God plainly spelled out in His Word, for I know this will aid them to grow more like Christ. As they are transformed by new knowledge from God's Holy Word, they are learning to live according to God's will. Applying His truth to our lives gives us freedom in a new and deeper sense. It's not just complying to some hard standards, but gaining holy ground in understanding what really works for our benefit in life.

Even as a counselor, I continued to learn more of God's Word and His standards, and especially how to apply His principles to my life. Daily, we grow in our walk with God when we study His Scriptures. My parents did not personally instruct me in the Holy Word during my growing up years, and that omission left me struggling to learn more in my young adult life. I always felt that hindered me from passing on more of God's wisdom to my own family.

Review:
There are two ways to approach life: by either living by God's standard or ignoring His Word. Compromising the truth leaves our lives empty shells with no substance. Indifference, instead of loving others, is showing up more and more. Veering from the truth has its consequences.

Closing Remarks:
We are influencing others by the values we hold.
We reflect our love for God by living by His principles.
God's standard is intended to keep us healthy and strong.
His Word is the way to what really works best in handling life.

Chapter Fifteen

FAITH, OUR SUPPORT

In life we use several words to describe faith: trust, belief, confidence, dependence, and assurance. Faith is the moving force in one's life, for it carries a real sense of trust and confidence in the source. We step out in faith and in full certainty of mind that something is true, that it will happen and/or will not fail. How greatly faith in God is needed in the Christian's life, so we can successfully walk closer to our invisible and mighty Creator. As life transpires, faith is a necessary ingredient.

> Now faith is the assurance of things hoped for,
> the conviction of things not seen.
> (Hebrews 11:1)

Q: On what support system do you lean? What is the importance of faith to the Christian?

A: During hard times, on what foundation do we base our lives? As we often walk through the valley of Baca or tears of sorrow, we need a support system, for we live in a world full of woes and troubles. In the Scriptures, Christians are reminded that *faith* must be at the center of our existence, for the apostle Paul proclaimed, "While we are at home in the body we are absent from the Lord—for we walk by faith, not by sight" (2 Corinthians 5:7). The author of Hebrews also declares, "without faith it is impossible to please Him" (Hebrews 11:6). Thus, faith is essential! Our belief and confidence is based on an invisible God, but real faith connects us with our unseen God by declaring our trust in Him.

There is a great difference though between walking by faith and walking by sight. God is a spirit. He lives in an unseen world—a very real world not experienced directly by us. God reigns in a world that holds forces and powers unknown to us. When we pray, we are praying to an *invisible* God that we cannot see, but when God answers our prayers we see *visible* answers occurring as things change. Then faith becomes a seeable reality.

Having faith means one believes in God and His ability to act on our behalf, as our Lord, not as our servant. As Christians we must come to the point of knowing that we can *trust* our Maker to be there when needed, and we need Him all the time. Our very walk with God will offer experiences that build our confidence in Him and His Word, once we step out in faith. His faithfulness brings proof that He can be relied upon. Thus, our convictions relate to the unfolding of God's truth to us both in His Word and in our life experiences, as God reveals His faithfulness.

Faith is at the base of our knowledge of God. Believing in God is our support beam. Merrill F. Unger, editor of *Unger's Bible Dictionary*, takes our understanding of faith one step beyond the common definition of belief or trust. He says, "Faith is not simply the assent of the intellect to revealed truth; it is the practical submission of the entire man to the guidance and control of such truth." When we accept the truths found in Scripture, we are acknowledging the trustworthiness of God's divine testimony and our willingness to do what God sets forth in His Word. Thus, Christians are proclaiming their fidelity to God by living lives based on the truth in the Scriptures, because God declares what's best for us in those holy pages. Christians are ever learning to be loyal and faithful to our Maker, the Lord God Almighty, as we come to understand more of His Word. The truth there stretches our growth and trust in Him.

When we accept by faith the contents of God's revelation, we become partakers of heavenly knowledge. Jesus said to His disciples, "To you it is been granted to know the mysteries of the kingdom of God" (Luke 8:10). God freely gives such heavenly wisdom to true believers (John 8:31-32; James 1:5). Christians gain more understanding of His truth as they grow in faith. The facts God has chosen to reveal go beyond what mankind can acquire by ordinary human effort and reason. Through the indwelling Holy Spirit, God inspires and aids us to understand His Word. Sometimes, in various places of the world, God may use "signs and wonders" to verify His Word by these events when the gospel is proclaimed. God honors even the smallest amount of faith to aid our growth in our knowledge of Him. Other times Christians must simply walk by faith and not by sight, but that trust pays off with a deeper relationship with our heavenly Father.

Faith offers us access to God. Faith also makes it possible to resist evil (Ephesians 3:20, 6:16). Christians can "fight the good fight" by keeping their faith (1 Timothy 6:12). The righteous live by faith (Romans 1:17). "Without faith it is impossible to please Him" (Hebrews 11:6). By turning to God, He will supply whatever is necessary in our Christian walk for support and spiritual battle. Instead of seeking various support groups outside the church, the Christian needs to lean on his faith and see what God will do.

Jesus declared to the disciples:

> If you have faith the size of a mustard seed, you will say to this mountain, "Move from here to there," and it will move; and nothing will be impossible to you.
> (Matthew 17:20)

> And all things you ask in prayer, believing, you will receive.
> (Matthew 21:22)

> All things are possible to him who believes.
> (Mark 9:23).

What greater gift can we give to God than our faith in Him? The Lord truly desires that we depend only on Him. Faith holds us up, and at the same time, bears the weight necessary to sustain us in our walk with God. Faith also proclaims our trust and confidence in the One who knows us best and the One who loves us the most.

Faith should be our core support in life.
Faith in the Creator expands our existence to an eternal sphere.
Without faith it is impossible to please God.
Our relationship depends on having confidence in our Maker.
With Him nothing is impossible.

FAITH, OUR SUPPORT

People put a lot of faith in every-day equipment both at home and at work. The adventurous will try new products and challenges without much thought. If it looks good and sturdy and even fun, people go for it. Sometimes just the manufacturer's label will cause someone to buy a new item, especially from a company that has been in business for a number of years. That is faith or trust in action, even though it may not be recognized as faith.

Clients have often come to me for counseling based on the word of a relative, friend, neighbor, or pastor, who passed out my information cards. They were coming depending on what was told them about my capability to help them work through their troubles. I always have felt that faith has brought them in and good results confirmed their faith.

Often people chose their dentist or doctor the same way, on the simple word of another who knows them. Once they experience how skillful and qualified the professional may be, they most likely will continue the relationship.

So it is with our relationship with God. He proves He is reliable when we step out in faith and trust Him. That first step is easier if we just remember that we are relying on the Creator of the universe who sustains it all.

We step out in faith daily in many areas, for life revolves around our trusting those things that make the world turn. Trusting this relationship or that object is important, because until you try something you do not know if it will work. Like riding on a ferry or a Ferris wheel or driving a car or tractor, we can't be sure how dependable those items will be, until we see them function.

Review:

Faith is an assumed, important ingredient in life, often not thought about and taken for granted. On what or on Whom do we base our trust? Submitting to the guidance of the revealed truth of God is faith. God proves His faithfulness by responding to our faith.

Closing Remarks:

Visible answers come when we pray to our invisible God.

He acts on our behalf when we trust Him.

Confidence in the One we cannot see deepens our relationship.

Depending on God never fails.

Chapter Sixteen

JESUS WEPT

How deeply the Creator of the world felt that day, as Jesus surveyed the sight before Him as He looked at Jerusalem. The people were held hostage by sin—heart-broken human beings headed for judgment. Christ's tears were not tears of joy. His tears were real sorrow, for He knew their coming pain. Overwhelming feelings of regret and passion consumed Him, for they had rejected their savior. Christ knew their circumstances could have had a different ending.

> When He approached Jerusalem,
> He saw the city and wept over it.
> (Luke 19:41)

Q: What is the significance of Jesus' weeping over Jerusalem?

A: One year I had the privilege of attending a magnificent Easter pageant. The most touching moment for me was when the man who portrayed Jesus wept over the staged city of Jerusalem.

Can you visualize the real Jesus with tears in His eyes on the hill looking down over Jerusalem? Do you see the extreme pain in those longing and sincere eyes? He knew a large portion of the people present was lost for all eternity. They were missing the real opportunity that He presented to them as their Messiah. Imagine what thoughts must have gone through His mind. He desired all men to be saved, yet the Lord knew man's own free will stood in the way of them accepting His gift of salvation. God would not coerce them to come to Him.

Jesus' countenance must have held only sadness, His shoulders sagging from the burden placed there by all mankind. The Lord's anguish was being reflected in His physical appearance, as His heart was being broken by man's rebellion against God and their own rejection of the truth. People He loved were missing the opportunity for a relationship with God. Before Jesus was the coming, painful crucifixion experience. The very reason for Him to be walking on the earth was to fulfill God's will concerning man's redemption. Jesus knew He must pour out His own blood to save those who would believe.

Yet, He wept: not for His own coming suffering, but for those who would not accept the way, the truth, and the life being offered by Him (John 14:6).

How often Jesus prayed for the people to hear His message of salvation is unknown, yet He often prayed. John, the Baptist, also had been sent before Him by God to proclaim the need to repent of sin and turn to the Messiah, who was among them. God had attempted to draw men to Him by sending the prophets before John, but the people did not hear their message. Israel was not listening. The coming of the Messiah had been prophesied just as He was then appearing, but they failed to comprehend (Zechariah 9:9). So Jesus was weeping for what might have been—a real relationship with God—that would mean being in the very presence of their Creator for all eternity.

His salvation offered so much more, for God desired to bless their present lives too.

Later on when Jesus hung on the cross and darkness had swept across the sky, a sense of total defeat spread outward across the people. Then those who realized that Jesus was the Son of God felt helpless and hopeless, for their master had been taken away that day. Those who did not know Him as their Lord remained suspended in time, for they had failed to realize this was a time of grace—a time when the very door of heaven had been opened by Jesus. All that was required was to believe in Him.

The same is true today. There are just two categories of people in the world: those who trust God and submit to Him, and those who continue to believe they can find their own way in life without surrendering their lives to Almighty God. They continue to stumble along alone, because they do not comprehend what Jesus' tears meant. How God longs to draw the lost to Himself, and they will not hear! How deeply He cares, and they do not comprehend!

We, who believe in Jesus, can rejoice that almost 2,000 years ago Christ did not remain held by death but was resurrected. His compassion for the lost has not changed since, for this is still the time of grace. Now before His second coming, the way to heaven remains open to anyone who can grasp how much He loves them, anyone who can visualize Him there with out-stretched hands and tears slowly running down His cheeks, and anyone who admits he or she is lost in his or her own self-importance and self-sufficiency. Jesus is inviting them in—to come home to heaven.

God does not desire to punish those who rebel against Him, as people deserve. He takes no joy in proclaiming judgment on a fallen world (Ezekiel 32:1-11). But His ineffable holiness and perfect righteousness demands justice against evil, and His wrath will come on a defiant world. God, who is wise and good, desires a real relationship with all those who are lost. He established His plan of salvation through Jesus, His Son. So if you need Christ as your Savior, now is the time to accept His offer (Hebrews 5:9). Jesus' tears that day then will not have been in vain. Now is the time of grace before His second coming and His judgment.

> Jesus' compassion extends completely to a lost world.
> He cares where we will spend eternity.
> He wasn't ashamed to let His tears flow for mankind.
> High on the hill, He shed tears for all those who need His salvation.
> Those present didn't recognize that the Messiah had come.
> They failed to claim what would give them peace with God.
> Today is still the day of salvation—a time of grace.

God has programmed us to release our sorrow by giving us the ability to cry. Tears are meant to relieve those inner feelings that come over us when disappointment strikes or some overwhelming change occurs. We may also shed tears of joy at some happy event, but not nearly as often as tears of pain.

The loss of my husband and the father of my children many years ago, still stirs deep feelings of sadness in my heart at times. Sometimes even actual tears will come. My feelings now are not so much for my own personal loss, for I have peace about that, but for the lack of opportunity for my children and grandchildren to know him as part of their lives. His genes and mine made them who they are. My sons and daughter would have gotten to know him better, and he could have been a real contributing part of my grandchildren's lives had he lived longer.

Bert was a man of compassion who opened his home and his heart to my earthly father. My husband never knew his own dad, because he died when Bert was just four years old. Yet, my husband invited my father to live with us just a year after we married. Dad had a need of a home and he lived with us until he passed away five years later. They became good friends, and I loved and respected them both deeply. Later, my husband, out of love, took in three of my nieces and a nephew when they needed rescuing from a dysfunctional home. My sorrow is due to the fact that he never got to share more of himself with our family, and many of our immediate family never had the opportunity to know him well.

Tears of sorrow rip our hearts to sheds at times, yet they help release some of the inner pain we are feeling. Life can be cruel. It doesn't discriminate about what it brings, or on whom such pain may fall. Yet, Jesus came to mend the brokenhearted (Isaiah 61:1). He understands the hurt we are experiencing, because He was deeply hurt by those who rejected Him. He felt their need for love, and for the forgiveness of their sins, and also of a restored relationship with God. Yet, His character would not allow Him to force them to accept Him.

In reality, the loss experienced is greater for the one who is doing the rejecting, than for the one rejected. But, the inflictors do not realize the truth of the matter until it's too late, if at all. Christ Jesus shares in our grief and wants to restore our lives, but we must invite Him to be a part. It is we who must do the inviting.

Review:

There is no question that Jesus loves deeply. As the Messiah, He faces rejection even now, as well as acceptance by some people. God does not force anyone to come to Him, nor does He overpower man's free will. Man's own rebellion often stands in the way of salvation. Each individual must decide.

Closing Remarks:

Jesus' tears were not for His own upcoming suffering.
He offered people a way back to God.
Accepting or rejecting the truth was their own choice.
Jesus wept for what might have been—that's love.
His tears need not be in vain if the lost believe.

Chapter Seventeen

THE BEAUTY OF GOD

The beauty of God is unlimited and all around us in many forms. The universe holds much mystery and wonder that draws one's attention to the Creator. The earth seen from an airplane shows its splendor. Nature blooms, dies, and blooms again each spring, and new life shouts the magnificence of God. The patience and compassion of an individual reflects that he personally knows God. As His consistency touches a life, that individual learns more about how beautiful God is.

> And let the beauty of the Lord our God be upon us:
> And establish thou the work of our hands upon us;
> Yea, the work of our hands establish thou it.
> (Psalm 90:17 KJV)

Q: Does your life convey the beauty of the Lord, as Psalm 90:17 suggests?

A: Author Henry Bosch, wrote, "He [God] is the fountain and source of all beauty." How true this statement is! As God's representatives here on earth, His beauty should be reflected through His people to the world. When the Lord's Holy Spirit indwells those who believe, then that inner transformation that occurs will manifest itself to others. The attributes of love, peace, and joy that God imparts are reflected outwardly in a believer's life. Further, the light of His truth shines through His people's character as the Spirit works in them.

During the springtime of April and May, the array of colorful flowers seem to reflect the Father's beauty everywhere, as the earth recovers from the harshness of winter. Each twig begins to shoot forth blossoms and new, brilliant, assorted colors of green, yellow, and red shine in the spring leaves. The mountains stand majestically and bright with newness, topped with the last remnants of snow on their white peaks.

New bird's nests are tucked in obscure places ready to hold fresh eggs that will bring new life in a short time. Even the rivers begin to flow beyond their existing banks, as they carve out new channels and reshape the tired old landscapes.

Unexpected blessings of birth are displayed as the cry of newborn babies, both human and animal, fill the air. While the morning dew on each blade of grass encourages growth of the reseeded and freshly fertilized lawns, people work at cleaning up their yards. Something deep inside is motivating them to make things shine again. The love of beauty is in the air!

Even the creeping vines that coil around their supporting trestles as they head upward toward heaven, declare the designing mind of God. For the watchful eye, there is much to observe of God's beauty display. This beauty appears in many orderly patterns and shapes. How lovely! How challenging! How glorious are the works of His hands, as new growth is seen pushing out and upward all over the earth. The mystery of new birth and renewal fills the air. Splendid is the beauty found in all of God's creation! This is just a small reflection of God's full glory that man has yet to behold.

Luke, the author of Acts, declared God is always nearby, and we should seek Him " . . . though He be not far from every one of us: for in Him we live and move and have our being" (Acts 17:27-28 KJV). Being in God's presence is true joy and personal satisfaction for those believers who encourage this relationship. They radiate some of the glory of their Maker, as other parts of creation also reveal its skillful designer. If you look closely at the details in creation, you will see the mysterious beauty of God's handiwork. The Almighty planned every detail so all things would function in harmony. The same is true of the human body. Many believers' countenance even will show a positive mental state from having been with God in their daily walk. His being nearby is reassuring to those to whom He has given essence and life. Seeking more of His nearness, which brings real harmony, should be our goal.

This beauty of the Lord, found in those who know Him, may be conveyed in the charm, grace, humor, patience, kindness, joy, love of music, goodness, and self-control of people, but mostly by showing simple compassion to others in a number of ways. Sometimes God's beauty is directed toward us when least expected. Other times, His loveliness comes from new, surprising sources, but always you know and see something special in the giver who reflects God's love. Let us all practice encouraging one another and lifting up those in our presence. When Christians do, they are spiritually growing more in the Lord, and the love of Christ is motivating them to graciously give more of themselves. Then others will feel the very compassion of Christ and know such love is coming from His followers, because God's love rules in the believers' hearts. The comfort and care they give out reveals how much God cares for all people. So, let the beauty of the Lord our God fill you, and spill over into the lives of others, for His fountain of love, joy, strength, and grace never runs dry.

> We want our work to be established and to count for something.
> Our legacy will count when our labor is done in love.
> Then the rich, mysterious beauty of God will be known to be in us.
> His delightful comfort and care will spill out to others,
> when we remain close to our God.

How good something, like a new dress, suit, couch or even a house, may look in the beginning right after it is purchased. It can be amazing! But in a short time, that brand-new look begins to change, as the item becomes worn from use.

Just the opposite is true of a believer. A man or woman, who gives his or her heart to the Lord, begins to change from the old person to a completely different person. Gradually, that person becomes more beautiful and reflects this change in his or her behavior. There is just something about such a countenance that is different—pleasing to look at, lovely to behold, and delightful just to see. The heart changes, their desires change, and even if they are old physically, their eyes and smile still express a difference in them. As God's Word penetrates deeper into the soul, that individual longs to be made completely new, washed of sin, and made white as snow.

I love to see such a change as God causes the poor, downtrodden, mourners, captives, and the brokenhearted to be made new again in spirit. People say, "Beauty is only skin deep," but that is not true of those who have given their hearts to God and have the promise of eternal life. The transformation is enduring—forever lasting.

I feel so overwhelmed with joy when I see a client begin to change who came feeling hopeless. The sessions may be many before there starts to be a gleam in his or her eye, but gradually the person begins to believe in himself or herself, believe in God, and realize the future can be bright and changed. Hope has been restored! Faith shows in a new trust in God. Love shines through their lives again. They are changed as the beauty of God comes over them.

Christians can also look forward to being more beautiful in heaven, as each believer absorbs some of God's glory, or radiant beauty, just by being in His presence. We will no longer bear the earthly image touched by sin. We will bear the heavenly image that radiates from God.

Review:

God can be known by what surrounds us in nature, for it reflects His glory. The details found in the artful order of creation also proclaim God's love of beauty. Such a great designing mind carefully crafted each and every item to work harmoniously. The patterns declare His efficiency.

Closing Remarks:

Being with God establishes a person's positive mental state.
God's beauty becomes a believer's to share.
This love of beauty that comes from God is a motivating force.

Chapter Eighteen

Priests of God

Christians have a responsibility to be priests ordained by Christ, as those who are set apart to minister to others. To really find personal satisfaction in life, we need to lay aside our own goals and strive to fulfill what God intends for our lives. By doing so, we reach great potential and purpose, because God has designed what is best for us as individuals. This is what Jesus expressed to His disciples when He said, "He who has found his life will lose it, and he who has lost his life for My sake will find it" (Matthew 10:39). Those who serve find the real treasures of life intended for them.

> And He has made us to be a kingdom,
> priests to His God and Father—to Him be the
> glory and the dominion forever and ever. Amen.
> (Revelation 1:6)

Q: What are some ways we can expand our role as priests of God?

A: There are four important ways we can enlarge our ministry to others as seen in the life of Jesus our Lord. While these suggestions are not the only avenues of service, they are: 1) *to be sympathetic* with those in need, 2) *to edify* by lifting the burdens of others, 3) *to comfort* those suffering, and (4) *to feed* the hungry and nurture the lost. Beginning with our brothers and sisters in the church; we, as God's chosen priests, need to deal gently with others while serving and fulfilling our acts of worship to God. All service that we extend to others is, in fact, a way of worshipping God.

Jesus took on a human body and nature so that He could personally function as our redeemer and high priest. By descending from heaven to live here, the Lord could then sympathize with all humans from firsthand experience. His work consisted of healing those with special needs, curing those with disease, casting out demons, and preaching and teaching the gospel of God's kingdom before He went to the cross as our savior (Matthew 11:5). Jesus went to the broken, the scarred, the lost, the imperfect, and freed them physically and spiritually. An Old Testament prophecy says of Jesus' followers, "But you will be called the priests of the Lord; you will be spoken of as ministers of our God" (Isaiah 61:6). We are called to serve as Jesus did while on earth. That is our glorious purpose as believers.

Jesus uplifted and edified the downtrodden by His full acceptance of the unclean sinner, no matter in what condition He found people. Healing the leper is an example of how He dealt with those who were outcast and considered incurable by society. The Lord literally restored the afflicted man with a touch (Matthew 8:23). Later, He was even known to be in the home of Simon, a leper. This revealed His belief in the uniqueness of each individual despite his repulsive, physical state (Matthew 26:6). The Lord sacrificially and gently opened His arms wide to the untouchable, and freely gave healing to all those in need.

Jesus also showed compassion to the lady who lost her son and was in the process of burying him, for He restored the lad to life and health, giving him back to the widow from the very grip of death (Luke 7:12-15). To the mother who was in mourning, great comfort, security, and hope were offered by this act of mercy.

Jesus fed people both physically and spiritually, for He knew they needed their inner "thirst" quenched, as well as their hunger for real food satisfied (John 4:5-24; Mark 8:2, 8, 16:21). People have the same needs today—to be given food for their bodies—but even more importantly, nourishment for their souls. When we teach the solid Word of God, the very principles of the Father feeds the minds and hearts of struggling people. Edifying people is part of our ministry. After His resurrection, Jesus challenged Peter to show his love for the Lord by faithfully feeding and tending the "sheep." All disciples and even non-believers need such loving care; as priests we are to offer such comfort to others.

As He rode into the city on Palm Sunday, the Lord was stirred with great sympathy for the citizens of Jerusalem. While some people proclaimed Him King and Lord, He wept over other's lack of understanding of *who He* is, and *what His visit* to earth really meant. This triumphant entry was a most touching scene, for some recognized Him as the Son of God, while others remained lost. Their rejection of the only way out of their despair brought tears to Jesus' eyes (Luke 19:37-44). His real desire was to gather the citizens of the great city under His protective "wings" of salvation (Luke 13:34-35). They could have discovered real, inner peace, but they failed to do so by rejecting the source—Christ Jesus, Himself.

If we, as His priests, will recognize those areas of service available to us, and show more *sympathy* and *comfort* to those who are struggling in life, then our personal ministry will keep expanding. If we were to share just one Scripture a day with someone with less knowledge of God's Word, then we would be *edifying* and *feeding* others as the Lord did. Being a priest for Christ is a marvelous privilege, but being priests also carries serious responsibilities! As priests, great opportunities are available in which we can express God's favor to others, and our actions bring His favor to us as well. Failing to use the opportunities keeps both us, and others, from experiencing God's blessings. As we gain more perspective from our own experiences and the study of God's Word, then we should show more empathy to others in need. We need to readily fulfill the role of priest and pass on more of His love. When we do fulfill our role as priests by serving our heavenly Father, our own hearts will be full of contentment and personal satisfaction.

> Being ordained as priests by Christ is a privilege.
> This position in the kingdom is not to be taken lightly.
> Being priests demands our full attention and commitment.
> Christians are not to neglect their work.
> Serving others comes from being sons and daughters of God.
> Serving in love will bring its rewards here and in heaven.

When I was growing up, I saw several of Bing Crosby's movies, and I remember that he played the part of a priest in some. It wasn't until years later that I learned of his personal connection with the Roman Catholic Church. Those were great screenplays that deeply impressed me.

At the time, I thought it would be something special to become a nun, but, of course, I didn't know how a girl became one. The concept was just a thought that remained in the back of my mind, but the desire wasn't strong enough to act on it so the wondering just remained there.

Later when I went to Bible college and began to seriously study the Scriptures, I discovered that believers in Christ Jesus already were called priests, not just men, but women also. This role was a surprise to me. All the people of God are now His priests. Christ Jesus is our High Priest, and because we now have direct access to God, Christians are meant to work with the Lord reconciling man to God. We are to administer God's love and grace to lost and struggling people.

God has given believers a position as priests in His kingdom and a ministry of reconciliation, an awesome responsibility to fulfill. Serving God in this ministry as His priests is a high honor and a real privilege. As we represent Him, we are to proclaim the excellency of God to those in need. That vague dream of mine to become a nun, so many years ago, materialized in another avenue of service as a God-ordained priest who counseled others. This avenue is simply another way of serving God fully.

Review:

To reach our full potential, we need to strive to fill our area of service that God ordained. Called to be priests, we as believers need to find and fill our place. We are worshipping God, if we do. As Jesus ministered to others, so are we to follow His example.

Closing Remarks:
God values even incurable and repulsive individuals.
Showing empathy and comfort is our responsibility.
The need for physical and spiritual nourishment is great!
We honor God when we fulfill our role as priests.

Chapter Nineteen

SPIRITUAL GIFTS

The Holy Spirit gives each Christian spiritual gifts. Not all believers have the same gifts, but these special talents and abilities are meant for the common good of the church to function efficiently. None are to be envied, but all Christians are to be encouraged to find and use their gifts for God's glory. Using our spiritual gifts for other people's benefit is a privilege that enhances us individually in finding our own true identity.

> Now there are varieties of gifts, but the same spirit . . .
> But to each one is given the manifestation
> of the Spirit for the common good.
> (1 Corinthians 12:4; 7)

Q: How do we discover our spiritual gifts and use them for God's glory?

A: Many people wonder, *how can I know what my spiritual gifts are?* Others declare with great conviction they have no gifts. While some believers continue to search for real meaning and purpose, they miss opportunity after opportunity to find fulfillment, because they fail to use their talents. God has given all Christians gifts; discovering them is our responsibility!

Living with purpose is really simple. We, who have accepted Christ as our savior, have been saved to serve (2 Timothy 1:9). Each of us has been given at least one spiritual gift to be used for the kingdom of God. Most have many more gifts than they acknowledge or realize indwells them (1 Peter 4:10). The author of Hebrews encouraged believers with these words, "And do not neglect doing good and sharing, for with such sacrifices God is pleased" (Heb. 13:16). Checking the list of spiritual gifts in the Scriptures is helpful in discovering where your interests are and what you can do to serve better (see 1 Corinthians 12:4-11, 27-28; Ephesians 4:11; Romans 12:6-8; 1 Peter 4:10-11).

To actively serve Christ, we need only to present the love of God to those around us as opportunities open up. Our own spirituality deepens when we minister to others. As we grow closer to the Lord and desire to reflect His great love to our community, we will find definitely more ways to serve. Serving others is part of growing in the grace and knowledge of Jesus Christ (2 Peter 3:18). The exciting thing is that we will discover more about ourselves, and our abilities, as we complete the tasks God gives us. We will discover we have more potential than we first believed, and we can try new ways to serve. God is often preparing us for something definite as we daily struggle to fulfill the task He has given us.

Once I watched a five-year old boy playing the drums on TV as if he were a professional performer who had been playing for many years. What a shame it would have been had this child not been allowed to perform because of his age, for thousands would have missed this blessing. While he was an exceptional, gifted boy, he was one person who was using his God-given talent fully for the benefit of others, and perhaps unknowingly influencing others. There is a perfect opportunity to serve in some way around each "corner," All we need is the eyes and heart of Jesus to see the need and fill it.

Each of us abounds in many abilities, even though we may not be aware of all of them. Some people can prepare nutritious meals, as Martha did, and invite guests in or take food to those in need; while other believers can offer transportation to the physically handicapped or those blind. By cleaning someone's house, the love of Christ may be shown with each stroke that removes the accumulated dust. Building a ramp may offer easier access to a disabled person's home. Offering advice to those struggling with financial needs or marital problems is another avenue of service; or just listening may be all that is necessary when someone is grieving.

We can use our physical strength or our intellectual capabilities to help others. Those simple acts reflect the kindness of Christ to others in need. Beyond these routine things, when Christians work as witnesses for Christ that is really His compassion at work reaching out to the lost. Visiting prisons or homeless shelters with the gospel brings troubled people a glimpse of hope that things can be better. Christ's saving love becomes the motivating force behind our actions. For it is Christ who radically changes our lives when He is invited in as Savior and Lord. As we are changed inwardly, God's love moves us to action and we begin to reach out and fill the opportunities before us. By His power we are transformed and become His servants who share His love.

Meeting the practical needs of others in various areas, and putting those needs before our own concerns, brings personal satisfaction to us and real comfort and hope to those who are suffering. The end result flows to both those serving, as well as to those being served. Our own sense of personal fulfillment and joy is made complete when we help others. Using our spiritual gifts puts us on the path that God wants us to find and to fulfill our own potential in life.

The abundant life that Jesus desires for us brings real contentment; and this kind of life is found only through the avenue of service. As we discover more of our spiritual gifts, our opportunities to serve expand right before our eyes. Jesus Christ came to serve others, and His life left a tremendous example for us to follow (Matthew 16:25; John 13:5). Let us rally around the struggling individuals, and in serving them find the spiritual gifts we possess. In doing so, we become living sacrifices unto God—serving, praising, and worshipping our heavenly Father.

<blockquote>
Spiritual gifts are valuable treasures from God.
Searching for our abilities and talents
draws us closer to the Lord Himself.
Used often, our gifts enhance our meaning and purpose in life.
As living sacrifices, we honor God when we serve others.
</blockquote>

Discovering my spiritual gifts was a challenge. The process took time as I grew spiritually. Gradually though, I realized I was gifted in discerning the facts. As I began working with clients to help those suffering from a number of different problems, I learned that discernment was truly my strongest gift. Discernment is a very important gift for the work I was called to do.

The ability for keen perception in a difficult situation is necessary to see clearly what the problem is and what areas one should attempt to change. When people are venting strong feelings, discernment aids the counselor to move the clients to see beyond the problem to a workable solution. Being able to judge the situation accurately is essential to bringing harmony and peace to troubled situations.

To get a couple, or even an individual, to concentrate on the total situation rather than on some hurt or disappointment takes time, patience, accurate information, and some real doing. People get so set in their own patterns that change is not easy. Working to move them to a higher level of understanding is an important goal for the counselor.

As I studied more of God's Word and gained my master's degree in theology, my ability to discern also increased. During those years of study, I also looked long and hard at the lists of the spiritual gifts given by the Holy Spirit as provided in Scripture. I saw my interests, and the areas where I desired to work more clearly, and began to focus on the direction God was leading me. Seeking more knowledge from God's teachings amplified this insight, helping me to become a better counselor.

Sometimes God simply uses this discernment to make me aware of someone in a crowd who needs help; other times it becomes clear that something needs my immediate attention and prayer. The Holy Spirit is the giver of gifts, and the Helper in our using those gifts, if we allow Him to function in our calling. He blesses our efforts to use our gifts to further the kingdom of God and to glorify Him. While I have other gifts and talents beyond discernment, this gift remains my strongest ability for the use of the common good of others.

Review:

If you want to discover your true identity, explore your talents and gifts, then use them for the common good of others—this is our purpose. Our spirituality deepens the more we complete our God-given tasks.

Closing Remarks:

From listening to the grieving to building homes, God can use us. Real compassion shows it cares.

Everyone needs hope and those who minister can give it.

Spiritual gifts are intended to aid us in our work, and to bring glory to God.

Chapter Twenty

OUR WEAKNESSES

Because our talents and personalities are different, as well as our educational opportunities, we personally are not adequate in all areas. But God made each of us unique with our limits and strengths! We should strive to improve and please God with what we are able to do with the gifts and talents He has given us. Our Lord only holds us responsible for what we are capable of doing.

> And He has said to me, "My grace is sufficient for you,
> For power is perfected in weakness."
> (2 Corinthians 12:9)

Q: What do we do with our weaknesses?

A: We all have weak areas in our lives. Some are physical, some emotional, and some spiritual matters, but all need personal attention to hopefully overcome. At times we tend to procrastinate, show favoritism, become fearful, complain a lot, become anxious, struggle with temptations, become prideful, even opinionated, and seriously rebel against others or even God.

There are just certain weak areas of our personality that tend to pull us toward failure. The devil likes to concentrate on those issues to hinder our functioning for God.

Jesus said, "The thief comes only to steal and kill and destroy" (John 10:10). This thief is the devil—the chief opponent of God. Often Christians fail to comprehend what Jesus was teaching His followers about our true enemy who wanders about seeking someone to destroy. The devil, called Satan (Revelation 20:2), will take our life if possible. But, when that does not happen, he seeks to use the weaknesses in our lives against us. He steals emotional peace and tranquility by causing stress, strain, and frustration. He may even drain away our physical and spiritual strength by a variety of means when we fail to turn things over to God.

One example given in Scripture is from the life of Samson. Delilah was a greedy person who was determined to obtain Samson's secret to his great strength. "She pressed him daily with her words and urged him, that his soul was annoyed to death" (Judges 16:16-17). Here is a case of the one closes to him, Delilah, using the information entrusted to her as a weapon to destroy Samson. She became the agent of the devil, for she betrayed Samson when he revealed his secret to her.

Samson was a man who had been set apart and consecrated into God's service from birth. But, he allowed his weakness for women to overcome his Nazarite vow to God. Instead of turning to God to gain command over the annoyance, he gave in and told his secret.

In the New Testament, Christians can learn from the apostle Paul how to handle weaknesses. Paul had a physical problem (what exactly is unknown), and he urgently prayed three times asking God to remove "the thorn in the flesh" (2 Corinthians 12:7-8). Whatever the problem, this "thorn" meant pain, discomfort, difficulty, and annoyance. But Paul never allowed it to control his life, for he turned the problem completely over to God.

Paul did not receive the answer to his prayer that he expected and desired, but God gave him something *more* and *better*. God gave him strength and grace to carry him on through the difficulty (2 Corinthians 9:8, 12:9). No matter what weaknesses we have to deal with, success to overcome those problems comes down to our free will and to our choices. We can choose to give the weakness to God—or not—then deal with the results.

Samson's way was to attempt to handle the event in his own strength. As a Nazarite consecrated to God, he should have first consulted God. Failing to do so, the consequences were that Samson lost the very strength that had made him powerful, because his might came from God. Paul on the other hand consulted his creator, sustainer, and provider. Paul learned that God's grace would carry him through his times of weakness. God's grace is always sufficient (2 Cor. 12:9). By His grace we can deal with our weak areas and allow Him to make us adequate.

Proverbs 3:25-26 says:

> Do not be afraid of sudden fear
> Nor of the onslaught of the wicked when it comes;
> For the Lord will be your confidence.

Based on this promise, weaknesses, trials, and personal difficulties all provide the opportunity for us to allow God's grace to flow through us to the world. In turn, God grants us strength to endure and overcome, while He is glorified.

None of us is totally adequate in life.
Yet God declares His grace is available.
He also provides the Holy Spirit to assist us.
The sufficient grace of God carries us through the problems.
When we reach out and accept God's generous grace,
His strength is more than adequate.

Speaking at women's retreats, church conferences, or before church assemblies was not my cup of tea in the beginning. I could easily relate to both Moses and Paul who neither one felt adequate. Even though I felt required to fulfill the role of a speaker when asked, I never felt comfortable before a large crowd. Working as a counselor one-on-one or with couples, and teaching a Bible class with fifteen or twenty people were more my comfort zone. Yet, God kept placing me up before larger groups as I grew in my faith.

As I shared some of my personal suffering and His overwhelming grace that carried me through the valleys of enduring pain, I could also share that His grace was sufficient. Not once when I was hit with some major event did God fail to love and support me through it all. His compassion and kindness always came in the amount that I needed.

Just recently, I was given the opportunity to share some of the marvelous ways God showed His love, some twenty-eight years ago, when I went through major surgery. A hurting individual had crossed my path who needed to hear about the faithfulness of God. God will reveal His power and control of our situations at our weakest moments in life. In the darkest times when we are suffering, the Lord proves His dependability. Those sad events turn into times when we get to know ourselves, and especially, our Creator better.

I can share that my weaknesses and limitations were times when God revealed His closeness. Several times when I was physically ill, I was called to respond to a personal need of one of my clients. Then the grace of God seemed to flow in and strengthen me to complete the task and help in a crisis. Those stressful meetings were more productive than other counseling sessions had been. As God told the apostle Paul, He proved to me that His grace is sufficient, despite my weakness.

Review:

While we all have our strengths, we also have our weaknesses. God has created our character with its strong traits. We are called by our Creator to use our talents for His glory and allow His grace to strengthen our weak areas.

Closing Remarks:

We handle best our weaknesses by God's grace.
Turning these areas over to God is best and we will see His marvels done.
God only holds us responsible for what we can do.
There is our way or God's way. Which is better?

Chapter Twenty-One

INEXPRESSIBLE JOY

When we allow God to be a part of our lives, He responds with His kindness and faithfulness. The Lord extends His best to His people. Like fresh air, His love and joy restores stale lives. This is the special joy that comes from God's salvation and a relationship with our Creator. Because it is deep-rooted in knowing our God, our happiness can be so great that our joy is beyond expression in mere words.

> For I will turn their mourning into joy
> And will comfort them and give them joy for their sorrow.
> (Jeremiah 31:13b)

Q: Will you describe the joy one has as a Christian and its source?

A: There is a vast difference between just an instant of happiness that one experiences in life from the everlasting *joy* that comes down from God. The Scriptures declare, "Every perfect gift is from above, coming down from the Father" (James 1:17). That's the source of such joy. Such joy is heavenly sent!

One morning a family member declared, "It's Friday!" as she revealed the sheer happiness that comes from realizing it is the last day of the work week. But, the everlasting joy in Christ Jesus is much deeper in dimension than a brief sense of relief that comes when one has completed some responsibility. The redemption found in Christ provides such joy. Sheer delight comes from being refreshed and made new again. When one's life is right with God by accepting His gift of salvation through Christ, one's whole outlook on life is changed. The old person becomes new. The destructive sins are gone. Our desires change to wanting to please God. There is personal joy and gratification that comes from our transformation and being allowed in God's presence.

As the Lord indicated to His disciples personally, Jesus desires His followers to have both joy and peace (John 16:24, 33). Later in Christ's intercessory prayer found in John 17, Jesus set forth what He knew to be an essential emotion for His followers: He asked God for His joy to be theirs. The Lord prayed earnestly and He had a deep desire for all Christians to be successful in their Christian walk. Part of His request was that we might experience the real joy that comes from knowing God. This passage in John declares the Lord's deep concern for Christians. In essence, He was praying for our joy to be full by our renewed relationship with His Father. Jesus wants us as Christians to have full gladness in our hearts—a holy gladness that comes from above.

In the Old Testament, David was a man who spent much time escaping from King Saul's plots to kill him. Many times he escaped actual attempts on his life. Yet David wrote several psalms of praise to God, those melodies springing from his lips when he was in hiding. While David's course was trying and tough, there was a deep delight within him from his intimate relationship and knowledge of God.

Nehemiah in the Old Testament also said, "Do not be grieved, for the joy of the Lord is your strength" (Nehemiah 8:10). Isaiah declared, "They will obtain gladness and joy, and sorrow and sighing will flee away" (Isaiah 51:11). The prophet Jeremiah stated, "Thy words were found, and I did eat them; and thy words were unto me a joy and the rejoicing of my heart" (Jeremiah 15:16 ASV). Paul in the New Testament proclaimed that the Corinthians would have "an abundance of joy" even in their afflictions (2 Corinthians 8:2). When we believe in Christ Jesus and love Him, we can experience "joy inexpressible" in our relationship with the Lord (1 Peter 1:8). As we study God's Word, increased spiritual insight results so "our joy may be made complete" (1 John 1:4).

True joy is a gift from God that comes as fruit of the indwelling presence of the Holy Spirit (Galatians 5:22). Allowing the Spirit to function within our lives permits that joy to surface and deepen within our soul. Christ's joy can fill a room with laughter or be reflected in just the look on one's face. In unexpected and often quiet ways, the joy of the Lord comes and strengthens us when we know we are right with God. The more we turn away from our selfish ways and turn back to God, the more real joy will fill our hearts. As we live in the love of Christ Jesus and extend His love to others, the result will be true enjoyment, or a deep gladness of heart manifested in our lives.

Real joy comes from acknowledging God as our Creator and respecting Him above all else (Psalm 128:1-2). Joy also comes when we trust our Savior and Lord and believe completely in His Holy Word (Proverbs 16:20). The kind of gladness and joy that only God can give comes especially when we obey Him.

Real everlasting joy is found in God alone (John 13:15-17; Psalm 73:25-28). The Almighty can hear the cry of our soul and fill that longing as no other. Our redemption brings us back into His holy presence, and extends to us His own joy. As we remain attuned to God's nearness, God's power, and God's Word, the wellspring of personal joy becomes very real, for God is the fountain of all everlasting joy.

> Our relationship with God brings great joy.
> He offers eternal life and prosperity to His own people.
> As our relationship deepens, our happiness greatly intensifies,
> and our desire to know Him better expands.
> One leads to the other until we experience complete joy.
> Our real joy in the Lord is inexpressible completely in words.

Mostly when we talk about joy, we describe the latest joyful circumstances we have experienced, not that inner knowing that comes from being right with God. But, real joy is coupled with an inner sense of peace and contentment. Whether in a crowd or alone, God's joy remains strong and gives a sense of security that extends beyond any situation. It's hard to explain in words that feeling of deep gladness and delight; it's just felt.

When I was called by God to be a counselor at a teaching conference, He allowed me to experience the pain and suffering of those who were sharing some of their struggles. This was an overwhelming experience that left me heavy-laden with deep sadness in my soul. I carried that feeling for several days. On Sunday one of the ladies in my Bible class shared a joyful event that made everyone laugh. I could join them all in their happiness, but at the same time, I held deep inside this overpowering sense of helplessness and a crushing feeling I could not get rid of. This emotion was the complete opposite feeling of real joy. God wanted me to know the pain of the brokenhearted and feel the sense of hopelessness of the downtrodden, so I would be moved into a new task with greater compassion. He revealed to me that I was to become an encourager and extend His comfort, as well as advice, to those in need. The God of all comfort was preparing me to be more sensitive, and have real compassion for those who were grieving for one reason or another. He saw the necessity for me to be more responsive with deeper understanding of the compelling needs of others. This feeling that moved me to an inward compassion for others, even though extremely strong, did not destroy my own personal sense of joy.

At other times in my life, I've experienced both deep feelings of joy and sadness at the same moment. The feeling of intense grief was strong that day, and joy was also present. Mixed feelings of sorrow and happiness are normal enough, depending on the circumstances. But, it's the joy of God that will see you through that valley of Baca. My own hope, courage and gladness were heightened by this experience that God put me through, for He was there with me. Our joy in the Lord increases as our relationship with God becomes closer and greater.

Review:

The stalest of lives become refreshed and joyful when a relationship with God through His Son is established. As the relationship deepens, so does the joy, which becomes inexpressible by the fullest of words. Happiness comes and goes depending on circumstances, but God's joy becomes new each morning and remains all day.

Closing Remarks:
Life gets difficult at times.
Knowing God makes all the difference.
A holy gladness of heart strengthens us when we are attuned to God and His blessings.

Chapter Twenty-Two

STUDYING GOD'S WORD

Fellowshipping with other Christians is vital to our life. As we associate with believers, we can be inspired and encouraged in our Christian walk. Also, the more we study God's Word, the more we can know God, who reveals Himself in its pages. Applying His truths to our lives is only possible if we know them. Studying the Word individually, and with other Christians, reveals the practical value of the principles that can aid our walk through life.

> All Scripture is inspired by God and profitable
> for teaching, for reproof, for correction, for
> training in righteousness; so that the man of God may be
> adequate, equipped for every good work.
> (2 Timothy 3:16-17)

Q: How do Christians benefit by regularly participating in a Bible study group?

A: Each person has certain basic needs deep within—to belong, to feel accepted, and above all to be loved. As we struggle to determine our purpose in life and gain a sense of security and personal worth, a proper perspective on things is necessary. Human beings need an authoritative source of wisdom to answer our questions and offer guidance. That absolute truth is found in God's inspired Word, which goes beyond human knowledge. To enhance our outlook on life, we need to see things from God's perspective. Thus, we need to study the Scriptures, both individually and with other believers.

The more one studies God's truth in the Holy Bible, the more apt that person will be to understand life from God's viewpoint. God has revealed Himself to us within the sacred pages, and He desires for us to gain heavenly wisdom by getting to know Him better. Therefore, the apostle Paul instructed Timothy to "Be diligent to present yourself approved to God as a workman who does not need to be ashamed, handling accurately the word of truth" (2 Timothy 2:15). We can only do that if we know the Scriptures. The King James Version begins that verse with "Study to show thyself approved unto God." A diligent person is an industrious and persistent person, one who is actively engaged in pleasing God by knowing and correctly applying His Word to life. Studying goes beyond just reading a passage, it means to ponder and to apply the principles and standards found there to our life.

The Bible has been provided by God to offer answers to life's problems and circumstances. As our minds become centered on what God requires of us, the truth enlightens our understanding and heightens our walk with the Lord. In studying the Scriptures, we make wonderful discoveries as the Holy Spirit teaches us and guides our thoughts (John 14:26). Surprisingly, real nuggets of knowledge and wisdom are found in the holy pages. You may be amazed to discover the more of God's Word you learn, the more there is to unearth. Getting together in small groups to study the Bible is an uplifting experience, as we examine God's promises, His challenges, His priorities, His principles, His warnings, and His ways.

Christians who come together in love, provide a support group for those who may be going through difficult times. In such a caring group, brothers and sisters in the Lord can share also the faithfulness and goodness of God they have experienced (Proverbs 11:14). People can talk openly about their needs, or lack of understanding regarding their problems, because they are among friends. They can pray for those who are facing tough decisions, or even offer from their own experience words of advice to those who are struggling. As members become affirming encouragers to one another, they will experience the unity of believers. This unity comes from a deep bond of love developed between Christ's followers and a deep knowledge of His Word. Studying the Bible together in homes becomes a time of seeking God's strength, guidance, and grace as prayers are lifted upward to heaven.

Gathering together to study God's Word is one way we put God first and also discover His best for our lives. Meeting together also offers us a time to be accountable, as we hear God's instructions spoken in love. Those we respect and trust are seeking only to strengthen our relationship with Christ, as they share openly and honestly from the Scriptures. It isn't their place to judge, but to openly encourage their brothers and sisters in the Lord to understand His Word.

God desires to stretch us beyond our old comfort zones by helping us become more obedient to Him. So our presence at a small Bible study group enhances our own spiritual growth above our daily devotions and Sunday church attendance. Being in a good Bible study group can kindle a profound love for Jesus. Time in His Word can deepen in our hearts a respect for God and His inspired Word. The Bible is true! The Scriptures come alive to believers (Hebrews 4:12). The Word is dynamic as it works to change and shape the individual. It discerns and judges our thoughts and intentions. The stories in the Bible are about real people with real problems like ours, and those souls who found real answers from God. In the written Word, God is speaking to sufficiently equip each man and woman "for every good work" (2 Timothy 3:17). We truly can learn from the examples in Scripture. Being in a Bible study group opens the door of opportunity to learn how to adapt to life in every stage of our existence. Because God has given us in His Word the truth necessary to deal with life's challenges, we can live a victorious and fruitful Christian life.

> To be good at anything, we must apply ourselves to
> know the principles and standards of that line of work.
> God has given us His guidelines for a good and holy life.
> His desire is to offer wisdom on how to handle our human
> existence and experiences, because He loves us.
> He doesn't intend to leave us alone to fend for ourselves.
> The Holy Bible is our guide to holiness.
> Studying with others opens the way for greater understanding.

Years ago, God started me out in a Bible study group of believers from several different denominations. I questioned why He placed me in such a variety of believers, but I learned that they held to a sound core of biblical teachings. This was a good training lesson that made me realize God had many believers among different churches. We gathered for several years, and our love for each other continued to grow.

Just recently, I met a couple as they were leaving a store I was about to enter, who had been a part of the original Bible study group. Our deep love for each other still remained, even though we hadn't seen each other for four years. The last time our paths crossed was at the funeral of the man who hosted our study. We talked for several minutes, catching up on how things were going, and that sense of concern and what our time meant before was still very present.

We each carried away from those sessions more than Bible knowledge, although learning God's Word was our main goal. Just knowing other believers, helped established a bond that we will carry into eternity. The group had shared their joys and sorrows, love and deep respect during those days. They had been there for each other when the pain was overwhelming in some cases. They rejoiced when several saw their need to be baptized, as a way of fulfilling Christ's commandment (Matthew 28:18-28).

Through all the spiritual wars that were extremely strong, and the intense victories over illnesses and losses of loved ones, our group prayed together and supported each other. God had also used that first group to establish me as a Bible teacher, as about three months after I joined, I was asked to teach the study. As I was attending Bible college at the time, this was a great learning experience for me that helped instill God's Word deep in my heart. You cannot teach what you do not know! Leading this group made me study harder.

Bible study groups are extremely important. Such meetings with other believers in small gatherings offer personal time to really get to know each other, something our society badly needs today. Details of joyful events and also times of suffering can be shared, and we can give or receive the support that is needed during our trials.

Review:

To see life from God's perspective, we need to know His Holy Word. His principles best help us navigate through life, but only if we know them. The Word is dynamic and full of treasures.

Closing Remarks:

God's truth enlightens us and heightens our walk with Him. We can live victorious when His Word becomes a part of us. Inspiration and encouragement comes from others when we are together.

The bond of love we gain will remain with us in eternity.

Chapter Twenty-Three

BELIEVERS MATTER

Do we matter to God? How important are we to Him? Our worth is reflected in the extent to which God was willing to go to redeem mankind. Without God's efforts to draw us back into a relationship with Him, we would have remained lost. Like sheep that have wandered away from the flock, people have wandered away from God's path of righteousness into the path of sin. Worthless and lost in our transgressions, our need for redemption could not be met any other way than by Christ's death on the cross.

> Who shall separate us from the love of Christ?
> For I am convinced that neither death, nor life, nor angels, nor principalities, nor things present, nor things to come, nor powers, nor heights, nor depth, nor any other created thing, will be able to separate us from the love of God,
> which is in Christ Jesus our Lord.
> (Romans 8:35, 38-39)

Q: Have you ever wondered how much we matter to God?

A: Today people seem to be at a loss to know how deep God's love is for them, how sensitive He is to our needs, and how much God desires fellowship with His people. As I sat down to write about this subject of just how much God really cares, the sun's warmth penetrated my dining room window. One of God's many ways of revealing He cares is through nature and the consistency of the sun and other natural events He designed for our benefit. How deep is His love? How wide and inclusive are His feelings? How really unlimited is the love of our Creator? How important are we to our Maker? All are questions that we ask ourselves, our friends, and even God Himself at times. We are curious about our real worth and our relationship with God.

I recalled at that same time that the recent gusty winds, rain, and even tornados had brought darkness, chaos, and hopelessness to those who experienced personal injury and property loss. Real damage to their homes and businesses and loss of lives left many wondering about life. Yet, such destructive forces are extremely small and insignificant in comparison to the harm that sin has done to man's relationship with God, for sin keeps man from knowing God's great love. Sinful rebellion is a barrier between God and man that remains until we discover God's way of restoring that much-needed broken relationship.

That same morning, some of the apostle Paul's words resounded suddenly in my memory. Found in his letter to the Romans, those powerful words express our importance to God: "He that spared not His own Son, but delivered him up for us all" (Romans 8:32 ASV). Those profound words brought back the picture in my mind of Christ hanging on the cross for our sins. God allowed His Son to die in our place that all who do believe might be reconciled to Him. Almighty God, who created the world, had not spared His only Son the agony of the cross, so we could benefit personally from Jesus' pain. He willingly allowed His Son to die in our place, which conveys how much mankind means to God. Christ gladly fulfilled the painful task, and said, "It is finished" (John 19:30). We have no way to comprehend the agony Christ endured because of our sins that caused Him to be separated from His Father and our God. Jesus died in our place voluntarily! So believers really matter!

As God has set the seasons in motion to fulfill His purposes for our planet, He also has set His great love in motion to redeem fallen human beings from sin by sending Christ to live on earth and die in our place. While here the Lord Jesus revealed the compassion of God during His ministry to the people around Him. Overwhelming affection was in Jesus' eyes as He walked among the sick, and His awesome love was felt in His healing touch. By His life, Jesus conveyed that people matter to God. Every place He walked, Jesus' compassion touched people's lives in miraculous ways.

Christ's very presence inspired the disciples to believe His words and trust their whole lives unto Him, because they came to know personally this transforming love. During His ministry, they experienced the Lord's forgiveness and grace, as He walked among them. Even God's love and sovereignty was heard in Jesus' authoritative voice as He taught them daily about God's kingdom. As Adam and Eve walked with God in the garden, the disciples walked with the Son of God while He was on earth, and personally experienced firsthand how deeply He cared for others.

Believers have left their homes, businesses, families, traditions, and religious practices to follow the Son of God. They do these things because they discovered the truth recorded by the apostle John: "For God so loved the world, that He gave His only begotten Son, that whoever believes in Him shall not perish, but have eternal life" (John 3:16). John later said, "God is love" (1 John 4:8, 16). Each step Jesus took revealed this passionate love of God. His ministry was love in action because Jesus was "the exact representation of His nature" (Hebrews 1:3). Once we give our hearts to God by believing in Christ, His Son, nothing can separate us from God's undying love (Romans 8:37-39). God's absolute love exceeds abundantly beyond what we can expect, hope for, or dream possible, for we truly matter to Him.

> We have a holy God, One who cannot put up with evil!
> Yet, our God was willing to sacrifice His Son's life for our benefit.
> Covered by Jesus' righteousness,
> God pours out freely His mercy and grace on us.
> Our worth is then completely changed from sinner to saint.
> God's enormous love conveys that we do matter to Him.

My love for God grew more and more as I studied the life of Christ Jesus. The longing to know more about the Son of God was extremely deep within me by the time I attended high school. It took some time, though, after my baptism, before I realized that the promised Holy Spirit was a real part of my life.

Christ had promised His Spirit to believers who trust Him, and He was true to His word when I gave my heart to Him. When I finally realized that His presence was really in me, I also knew that Christ was walking with me, as He had done with the apostles. His indwelling presence was not the visible appearance we often desire, but Christ was real and within my being. That invisible Spirit guiding my thoughts and actions was something I felt.

The Holy presence became stronger and He made Himself known in a number of ways over time. Sometimes He spoke directly to me, while other times, the confidence I felt leading a Bible study group, teaching at a retreat or conference, or the very depth of my prayers in a crisis moved me to know I was out of my personal depth of knowledge and wisdom. Someone wiser and more powerful was involved in inspiring me, as words came from my mouth that surprised even me. I came to understand, too, that the outpouring of God's power and grace in trying times was an answer to my prayers, and the amazing results were brought about by the indwelling Holy Spirit.

Christ also promised not to forsake or abandon His people. As believers, we learn the faithfulness of His reassuring pledge when we come to know that the Holy Spirit is real and lives in our hearts and souls. Because I can rely on the presence of the Holy Spirit, I know that I matter to the Lord, as do other believers!

Review:

Every aspect of our life matters to God, who desires a relationship with the people He created. The willingness of God to allow His Son to die in our place reflects that believers have worth in God's eyes. We are not insignificant or worthless!

Closing Remarks:

Love in action brings results.
Jesus willingly proved His love for mankind on the cross.
Never doubt that we are important to our Creator.
Once a believer draws near to God, His great love engulfs him or her, never letting go.
The Holy Spirit's presence within us is living proof that we matter to God.

Chapter Twenty-Four

WALKING WITH GOD

Walking with God is the key to having a successful, satisfied life. His guidance directs us to the best life has to offer. The Lord knows our talents, abilities, and interests, and He will show us the way to a meaningful life that returns more to us than what we give. Our intimate walk with God will surpass all other relationships, when we pursue a lasting closeness with the Lord.

> They heard the sound of the Lord God
> walking in the garden in the cool of the day.
> (Genesis 3:8)

Q: How can Christians improve their walk with God?

A: Many years ago in the Garden of Eden, God came to walk in the cool of the day with Adam and Eve. In a place filled with beauty and peace, God offered them complete fellowship with Himself. God had planted the garden, and He placed within it trees that were magnificent to look upon and which produced excellent, edible food. God had placed Adam there as the gardener to cultivate and maintain this perfect paradise. God chose to reveal Himself there in the beginning to mankind by a close personal walk with both the man and the woman (Genesis 2:8, 15, 3:8). Truly that scene creates a wonderful, awesome picture of what God Almighty desires for those He created.

Before they succumbed to disobedience and sinned, both Adam and Eve had a special relationship with God, their Creator. We are not told in Scripture just how long they enjoyed this relationship before it became shattered. Think what it must have been like to hear the sound of God's footsteps as He came into their presence in the garden. There are no words to express the sheer joy and anticipation that wells up within the heart at the thought of being in God's presence. What a privilege it will be to be face to face with our Maker! But, our first parents failed to heed God's command, and they lost that unique relationship for their sin separated them from our Holy God (Isaiah 59:2).

Years later, while on earth, Jesus also walked many miles with His disciples. He often returned to a special place called the Garden of Gethsemane near the foot of the Mount of Olives (Luke 22:39). Jesus withdrew frequently to pray to our heavenly Father in seclusion in this tranquil place, taking the disciples with Him at times. To get to the garden retreat, Jesus had to cross the Kidron ravine, east of Jerusalem. This was a valley that had been used as a place to dump discarded idols, and in Josiah's day it became a common cemetery used for burials (2 Kings 23:6).

The night before His crucifixion, Jesus crossed over the area to commune with God in prayer, and He became physically strengthened by angels there in the garden. His life's journey ended in prayer, which empowered Him in His hour of need to be the One who was able to fulfill God's will on the cross. Jesus had come to bridge the gap between God and man. Sin had caused permanent separation; Christ Jesus was offering a way back. Unlike Adam and Eve, Jesus realized His personal need for God's grace to sustain Him as He fulfilled God's purpose for Him here on earth—to provide a way across the valley of death to a place of life. God had given Jesus instructions, and by heeding them, Jesus completed His awesome task. He died on the cross, but was raised to life three days later.

The Lord illustrated the need to cross the valley of death by walking through the Kidron valley. This scene is true for all Christians too! We must cross through the valley of death by walking with Jesus, who covers our sins. If we heed God's instructions in the Scriptures, we can complete our journey and gain eternal life. We can complete also the specific task God has called us to do while on earth, making our daily walk with God pleasing to Him.

God has given us instructions in His Word how we are to walk with Him. In Leviticus 26:3-12, God gave to the Israelites a summary statement of what is needed, and the results of such obedience. God will pour out His blessings upon His people when they keep the Sabbath, show a reverence for His sanctuary, walk in His statues, and keep His commandments. God will turn toward His people, not away from them, when they are obedient, and He will confirm His covenant with them. The Lord will also dwell among them. God declares that He will sustain His people who are faithful. God clearly says, "My soul will not reject you. I will also walk among you, and be your God, and you shall be My people" (Leviticus 26:11-12). They knew firmly what was expected. They were to live by His Word and God would empower them as He walked with them.

Under the New Testament covenant, God has covered us with grace, and offers more grace, that we may honor the same above instructions. The Lord will be there to instruct us, protect us, provide for us, encourage us, and direct our paths, if we remain faithful. As our God, He will meet our needs (Philippians 4:19). These are reassuring promises from God for His faithful people, but His warnings also follow to the unfaithful and disobedient.

Jesus also extended a promise to those who do not soil their garments with sin, when He declared, " . . . they will walk with me in white, for they are worthy" (Revelation 3:4). This is a promise of an eternal walk with the Lord for those who are faithful to Him. To remain faithful, recognize each need and turn to the Father in prayer for support as Jesus did. And continue to make God's will your own by studying and applying His Word to your life.

If we follow Jesus' example of turning to God in prayer, and we follow God's counsel found in His Word, then we will overcome life's temptations and not fail as did Adam and Eve. They did not consult God but hid themselves, as a result of their behavior, when they heard God approaching. Their sin caused them to feel ashamed. Then God drove them from the Garden of Eden—the paradise He created for them, and no longer walked daily with them. They lost that intimate relationship. When we remain faithful to God, we will be walking with God each day and not be separated from Him. This close, personal friendship with God comes from following His instructions, which pleases Him.

Walking With God

God desires to have a close relationship with us.
Our sin breaks that desired connection.
Our guilt causes us to want to hide when God approaches.
We can only renew that closeness through Christ
by accepting His unconditional love.
We can improve our walk with the Creator by
faithfully pursuing our relationship with Him through obedience.

One day my husband and I went to Ross Dam near the tiny town of Diablo here in the state of Washington for a scenic tour of the area and an early dinner. We had to wait for the large freight elevator to descend for us to go up to the level of the lake, and take a boat ride out to the massive structure.

As we boarded the platform and began to ascend, I turned to look at the grassy, green valley below, and immediately I felt the overwhelming presence of God engulfing me. Gazing at this beautiful part of His earth before me, I knew for the first time a real sense of God's sovereignty. The realization of the earth and everything in it being His property was as tangible that day as the giant boards beneath my feet, lifting me upward. It was no longer an intellectual understanding. The awareness of His presence was so strong it seemed touchable. Only a few moments passed, but in those fleeing minutes it was as if time stood still while God got my full attention. Beauty, peace, harmony, and contentment were all mine, as He briefly touched my life in a profound way. What a joy to feel such reassurance and closeness with the Lord! He was real and walking with me.

Strolling in any one of the beautiful gardens that can be found in or near our cities can give us a sense of this same total peace. And the awesome awareness of God found in the pure and natural surroundings in the national parks across our nation can be just as inspiring.

That serenity and sense of His presence here on earth is only a slight awareness of what living with God in eternity will be like. Yet the experience here and now is overwhelming to our senses. Experiencing being with Him is pure joy! In the Garden of Eden, God walked with Adam and Eve in the cool of the day. What I experienced at Diablo made their experience more real to me. Those days were for Adam and Eve a time when they could enjoy total fellowship with God and were engulfed in an intimate relationship with their Creator. They must have known pure pleasure from being in His presence as they journeyed throughout the place God had created for the first man and woman to live in and enjoy. Their time of communion with Him was a harmonious time of perfection, when nothing separated them from that special togetherness.

I've had other special moments when I knew God was with me. Sometimes those encounters came as a direct result of my asking God in prayer if He was with me. Other times, God chose to express His presence without my needing to ask. Once near a town called Loveland, I could feel His nearness when I took a break from driving on one of my trips. That simple name elevated the experience for me. God often reveals Himself when we are exhausted, discouraged, or in special need, but sometimes He just loves to make known His closeness for its part of His nature.

God also has given us the freedom today to come into His presence and be His children and friends. Jesus refers to His disciples as brothers if they follow His commands. Even though we live in a fallen world, which isn't like the first garden at all, we can be friends with Christ, and through Christ we have full access to God. Believing in Christ opens the way for us to experience our own garden time with God.

Review:

Walking with God is an awesome way of knowing the One who loves us most and desires what is best for us. His tangible presence uplifts and inspires us to live a holy life. His friendship is everlasting to those who trust Him and turn to Him.

Closing Remarks:

Our life becomes the most meaningful when God is a part of it.
Walking with Him is our choice to make.
For a unique relationship, establish a friendship with God.
It's an awe-inspiring privilege to know God is close by.

Chapter Twenty-Five

REMAINING FAITHFUL

The focus of our life will reap results, good or bad, depending upon whom or what we place our focus. Sometimes the circumstances of life are hard to bear, and they make us question just what should get our attention first. Time declares the faithfulness of God. It's important to recall all He has done for us in the past as it adds depth to our life. Knowing our God personally makes being loyal to Him easy despite our circumstances.

> My eyes shall be upon the faithful
> of the land, that they may dwell with me.
> (Psalm 101:6)

Q: What does it take to remain faithful to Christ until the end of our life's journey?

A: When life is not complicated and reasonably stable, Christians can easily remain loyal to Christ. When the difficulties begin to pour in, questions and doubt arise that can damage our relationship with the Lord. Michael Fanstone said, "The true depth of our faith is tested when problems arise." Very true are his words!

When we take our relationship with Christ Jesus seriously, there will be problems, testing, and pressures to deal with in life. God allows our faith to be tested in various ways. How real and how deep our faith is will be demonstrated in how we react in difficult times.

Jesus, in the book of Revelation, said, "Be faithful until death, and I will give you the crown of life" (Revelation 2:10). His promise of life hinges upon our full and complete commitment, despite what we may be called to endure. The Lord also told His disciples, "It is inevitable that stumbling blocks come" (Luke 17:1). So don't be surprised when things get rough, or get discouraged to the point of giving up. God promised that we would not have to endure more than we can bear, for He will provide our strength (1 Corinthians 10:13).

The real answer to handling life's problems is to realize there is a war to be won, but, as Christians, the Lord is with us. This truth unfolded in the Old Testament days when the Lord spoke to Gideon. God said, "The Lord is with you, O valiant warrior" (Judges 6:12). Gideon served God as an Israelite judge for forty years. We must remember that we are not alone in life's struggles, and we are truly in the middle of a spiritual battle, which really belongs to God. The battle is between good and evil. We are merely His instruments in this war.

Christ Jesus associated prayer with strength, and the means of escape. He said, "They ought to pray and not to lose heart" (Luke 18:1). Referring to difficult happenings in the end times, the Lord proclaimed that believers should "straighten up and lift up your heads" (Luke 21:28). Looking up keeps our focus on God, not the problems. Further, Christ declared, "Keep on the alert at all times, praying that you may have strength to escape all these things" (Luke 21:36). His instructions were to stand up, be alert, and pray about matters. Strength would then come from God. While on earth, Jesus Himself sought time to pray and be alone with His Father, never allowing the demands of life to destroy His source of strength (Luke 5:16).

The apostle Paul was able to declare, "I have fought the good fight, I have finished the course, I have kept the faith" (2 Timothy 4:7). As an apostle for Christ, he had gone through many hard times: beatings, shipwreck, imprisonments, and even stoning, yet he had survived. Thus, Paul had learned that we need a time to talk with God and listen intently to His instructions, for from God comes the power to endure. Paul makes this clear when he wrote to the Colossians, "Devote yourselves to prayer" (Colossians 4:2). When life begins to press in, keep time for communicating with God as your top priority. Do not be weighed down with the worries of life, but pray that you may have His power to endure. Experiencing God's enduring strength when we are weak shores up our faith in God, and helps us to remain faithful to Him.

Don't get sidetracked by deception—one of the greatest methods used by our enemy, the devil. But structure your whole life on the principles of God found in His Word, for the truth is strong and supportive in our walk. The apostle Peter proclaimed those people who are untaught and unstable distort the Scriptures, "to their own destruction" (2 Peter 3:16). Learn to discern the truth by studying and memorizing Scriptures. Knowing the Scriptures is the sure way of protecting ourselves when we are under attack from the enemy. This is the method Christ Jesus Himself used when Satan tempted Him.

Ask the Lord for His grace to carry you through, for His grace is sufficient, as Paul had learned. This marvelous servant of Christ expressed, "When I am weak, then I am strong" (2 Corinthians 12:10). He had discovered firsthand how sufficient God's grace could be. The psalmist also wrote, "My flesh and my heart may fail, but God is the strength of my heart and my portion forever" (Psalm 73:26). These were men who had been tested by life's severe problems and had come out on the winning side. They survived, because they used the strongest weapon—God's truth.

God has called us to be witnesses for Him. At times this involves a great battle between good and evil. He has asked us to live according to His moral standards. This may mean we will face strong opposition. But by total submission to God's will and complete dependence on Him, we can endure whatever may come along. Remaining faithful unto the end to the one sovereign God, who loves and cares for His own, happens when we are obedient and trust Him to supply what is necessary for us to endure. A humble, yielded, and trusting believer adheres to the only true source of life, God Himself. The faithful follower of Christ clings with confidence, not to himself, but to God alone. When we believe in God, adhere to His promises, remain loyal to Christ, His Son; God will claim us as His own children, and He remains with us every step of the way.

<blockquote>
Know there is a battle going on around us.
Sometimes we are called to confront the enemy.
Believers though are never alone.
Trusting God brings us the power to endure.
The truth will set us free when used.
The end will bring the crown of life to the faithful.
</blockquote>

As a counselor, seeing clients who came for advice taught me that life is full of all sorts of problems and struggles. The clients were so focused on the troubles they faced they could not see life from any other perspective. Yet God knows the whole picture and sees things in their true relationship to the other parts. My job was to get people to view life more from God's perspective and not exaggerate the importance of earthly trials, even though they may be great.

Our enemy, the devil, delights in keeping us focused on our problems. If he can keep us distracted from our source of strength, than we will become lost in the problem and unable to change direction. His goal is to destroy our relationship to God and our ability to serve the Lord in His plan for our life. The battle between good and evil started a long time ago, when the devil attempted to usurp the Lord God Almighty's rightful place of authority. This battle will continue until the Lord Jesus Christ returns and sets up His millennium kingdom.

Our vision now while on earth needs to be on eternal things, holding to the truth that God is sovereign over the whole universe. Although the battle may touch our lives, we must not become discouraged and limit our focus to what we are currently going through. We need to see each struggle or problem as an opportunity to learn what God knows will enhance our spiritual growth.

The reign of God is vast, beyond our imagination! We have before us a great opportunity to be a part of bringing others into His kingdom and experiencing with them the goodness that is there. We have to look beyond the moment of pain and suffering we may be enduring, and see what more God has in store for us. The battle may be hard, but God Himself assures the victory.

Review:

Where do we put our focus? How deep is our faith in God? The Lord Jesus called us to full commitment to Him. Remember, we are not alone in life's battles. Don't look at the problems; stay focused on God. He is our source of strength.

Closing Remarks:

Don't let life's worries weigh you down.

Pray for the power to endure.

We can discern the truth when we know the Scriptures.

Our commitment to Christ results in the Lord faithfully watching over us through all life's problems.

Chapter Twenty-Six

BEING TRUTHFUL

Truth is concrete, actual, and real. It remains true, exact, and accurate—something we can trust! Also, a man's word shows his character and worth. Does he speak with truth or with false words? Each word spoken leaves its mark for happiness and joy, or sorrow and pain. Untruthful words have a way of coming back to hurt the one who speaks them. Real truth is based on God's standard found in His Word—the absolute truth and divine authority for life.

> He who speaks truth tells what is right,
> But a false witness, deceit.
> There is one who speaks rashly like the thrusts of a sword.
> But the tongue of the wise brings healing.
> Truthful lips will be established forever,
> But a lying tongue is only for a moment.
> (Proverbs 12:17-19)

Q: What is the importance of being truthful?

A: The biblical concept of being truthful is set forth by Jesus when he declared, "If you continue in My word, then you are truly disciples of Mine: and you will know the truth, and the truth will make you free" (John 8:31-32). First, Jesus is indicating that truth is a mark of being His disciple, and secondly, freedom comes as a result of truth. In a world that struggles with being truthful, that statement is full of reassurance and inspiration. Knowing whom to trust is difficult.

The opposite of speaking the truth and having its freedom is being in real bondage. This is true for those who are prone to lie, continue to lie, and have not accepted God's Word as their ultimate guide. They cover one lie with another. Lying also indicates a person has not accepted, nor holds respect for, the lordship of Christ Jesus, who proclaimed truth while on earth. People who lie do not want to be under His authority, but hold on to their own self-centered lives and destructive ideas.

Christians should not be deceived into believing what was outlandishly once proclaimed on a television talk show. It was said, "Lying is sometimes appropriate." Whether one evades telling the truth by not volunteering the full information, or conveying what is commonly referred to as a so-called "white lie," such behavior is for self-serving reasons of common deception, and it claims justification for the conduct in question. Just because lying maybe practiced by others still doesn't make it the right thing to do. Giving a hearty approval to the practice of lying is a shameful and hurtful act of behavior—just another way of sinning.

When a person becomes a Christian, the old nature of man is replaced with a new nature. God gives a believer a new start in life. The slate is wiped clean, so one can begin fresh and renewed.

If we try to live life in our own strength, then the old nature remains in control. Since the character of a man is reflected in his word, being truthful shows one is living by the new nature. Lying is allowing the old self to practice its evil ways; untruthful words keep the Holy Spirit from aiding our walk with God (Colossians 3:9).

Further, there are consequences to dishonesty! One lie will lead to another and another lie, until a person's conscience becomes dull and unable to discern what is right. His or her credibility becomes questionable. If a man's word cannot be trusted, he has lost his reliability. He is making excuses and failing to take responsibility for his own conduct. The same is true of a woman. Lying simply cultivates the seed of distrust in any future relationship, and one's reputation is permanently damaged many times over. No matter how painful the truth may be, absolute truth is far better than a lie.

Jesus also revealed the source of all lies when He informed the Jews regarding the devil that "there is no truth in him . . . for he is a liar and the father of lies" (John 8:44). Who would be proud to be related to the father of lies? Yet, many are living it more than they realize. Those who do lie become the very instruments of the devil (see Romans 6:11-16) whose goal is to destroy people by deceit. Like a roaring lion, he lies in ambush to devour even an innocent, naive child. We are to always be on the alert and resist this evil one (1 Peter 5:8).

A contrite liar needs to be pardoned for his or her sin, as much as anyone else needing forgiveness for sinning. But, only when genuine repentance accompanies an open confession of sin can there be real healing in his or her relationship with God, and others. Facing the truth brings freedom from the bondage of sin, and it may even reestablish relationships. If there is no forgiveness by others who are hurt, this does not always happen.

What impact will your life have upon those close to you? Will it be a depressing influence resulting from bad behavior full of lies, or will it be a strong influence for good, because you held to the truth? Can other people depend upon your word? Do you offer a beneficial influence in turbulent times? Do you extend to others a sense of comfort, hope, peace, and love? And, do you, by your own life, compel people to tell the truth? These are tough questions that need answering.

Being truthful means one must render reality consistently and accurately in life, rather than falsely play games with the facts and lives of others. As true believers, we must learn to draw strength from Christ's grace and His truth. His strength will see us through life's circumstances, if at no time we rely on lies. Humbly depending on the Lord Jesus makes us overcomers who, as His disciples, have learned to be responsible for our actions. Further, as believers, we should claim His Word to be true to life and necessary in all situations. Standing for the truth brings glory to Almighty God too, who is our Father in heaven and the very essence of truth.

> As Christians, standing for the truth is essential.
> We represent our Holy God by our words and actions.
> When we stand before God, Christ will claim
> those who are truthful.
> The truth of the Lord is everlasting,
> And His Word keeps our hearts clean from the
> evil that lying devises.

When I worked as a counselor being truthful was painful at times for those who had to hear the truth, but it was essential. I had to learn early on in my work to be gentle and firm, although it wasn't always easy. Those struggling with problems and conflicts had to recognize what was causing their problems, and be urged to make changes. I based my advice on the truth in God's Word.

Once the mother of a daughter who had had an abortion came to discuss the matter. The mother was laboring emotionally over the event. She was leaning toward compromising the truth of God on the matter, because of her love for her child. And, she was seeking approval for her way in handling things.

When someone we love makes a mistake, we tend to overlook the error or offer excuses that hold her blameless. This doesn't aid our loved one in facing her choices and the consequences, nor does it help her to grow in her walk with the Lord. There will be consequences that she has to deal with. Sadly, the sense of guilt can be devastating!

While raising my own children, problems occurred that had to be dealt with. Finding out the truth was hard at times. The old nature wants to lie and cover up the mistakes, so the struggle to stand for the truth becomes great as a parent helps the child. Dr. Dobson's advice to administer "tough love" comes in handy when raising children. Yet, adults have to know the truth and then explain it to the younger generation, while living a life that shows how important truth is. If we don't, the errors continue to multiply and the individual loses ground, making it hard to regain this feature in his walk with Christ through life.

Review:

Our words speak loudly about our character. Are they helpful or harmful or hurtful? We can offer healing through our words, instead of deceit. Christ's disciples have freedom because they know the truth. The true character of a man or woman is reflected in his or her words.

Closing Remarks:

Will the old nature or the new nature reign?

Can we rely on a man's word, or is his reputation damaged?

God's standard is absolute truth.

Each word spoken leaves its mark.

Chapter Twenty-Seven

VISIBLE GLORY

Our attention is drawn toward those who are radiant and joyful. In most situations, this brightness and cheerfulness seems to flow outward and generously toward others. Without the awareness of their own appearance, believers can reflect an overwhelming sense of delightful presence to those around them. Something about their countenance is different despite life's situations. It conveys a sense of contentment and well-being that others lack. People may not understand this visible radiance, but they want it.

> Therefore, if anyone is in Christ, he is a new creature; the old things passed away; behold, new things have come.
> (2 Corinthians 5:17)

Q: What is the greatest visible display of God's glory seen in His people?

A: Each springtime, God refurbishes the earth with continuous rains to renew the established life all around in nature. The

Scripture says, "He waters the mountains from His upper chambers; the earth is satisfied with the fruit of His works" (Psalm 104:13). Fresh, pure water flows rapidly and offers an ever-rich means of essential support for the whole earth's needs. God is the true source of "living water" for all His creation, not just nature alone (John 4:10, 14). He readily supplies all that is necessary to rejuvenate and sustain His great works, including His people. The changes are noticeable to those who observe their surroundings and His children.

Before He departed the earth, the Lord Jesus told His disciples that those who believe in Him would receive the indwelling presence of the Holy Spirit. Something special happens then to cause a vast change in a believer who surrenders to the Lord. Those who receive the Holy Spirit, according to Jesus' words, receive "living water" that flows outward to those around them (John 7:38-39). This Helper is intended to fill the spiritual void in man, which came about as the result of sin, causing man's separation from God. Jesus revealed that it is the thirsty man who will be satisfied with the Holy Spirit's presence.

The filling that occurs at a person's rebirth produces a fountain of living water that continually flows from his inner being. For this to happen, a spiritual need must be recognized by the sinner. Referring to the believer, Jesus said, "From his innermost being will flow rivers of living water," (John 7:38b). Not only does inner transformation happen to those who follow Christ Jesus, but this brings about a visible change outwardly in the life of those who believe.

As God supplies the earth when it needs moisture and replenishing, so does the Lord extend to the believing person that which will quench his inner thirst and invigorate him. But, only the Holy Spirit can revive that spiritual part of man.

This vital part was dead because of sin; then the inner man is refreshed and made new with eternal life by the Spirit, when we give our hearts to God.

As energetic water comes down from heaven from God, every place the rain touches experiences renewal. When this life source touches the believer, this also produces the fruit of the Holy Spirit within each person. Renewed life graciously and continuously flows down from heaven and outward to others through the dedicated Christian. Love, joy, peace, patience, kindness, goodness, faithfulness, gentleness, and self-control are meant to radiate outward to others (Galatians 5:22-23). The Lord is "the fountain of living water"—the source that supplies this visible change (Jeremiah 2:13).

The greatest visible display of God's glory in His people comes when the Christian allows the Holy Spirit to shine forth the happiness, joy, contentment, love, and peace they have found in God. Christians are not just receivers, but they are intended to be givers as well. God renews believers' lives so they can serve others by helping with their needs. When they do, God's own radiance and glory shines through them.

God intended the living water of life that comes from His throne to be active, moving, and imparted outward to others, so those in need will know His grace and mercy. Touching the lives of believers and non-believers is simply *agape* love at work, edifying and encouraging wherever there is a need. God's Holy Spirit is at work in His people, and His fruit flourishes, for God's love is not allowed to become stagnant in the one who receives the renewing gift of life.

God uses the same sustaining power in us that He uses to operate the vast universe in which our earth is a minute part.

This process is expressed by the apostle Paul when he said, "If we live by the Spirit, let us also walk by the Spirit" (Galatians 5:25), for from Him comes the power to overcome. God has given the believer new life so we can successfully live for Him. We do this through the power of the Holy Spirit. Then the Almighty expects us to share what we have received—the message that He is the fountain of living water and all essential things. The Holy Spirit will empower us to respond and share with others what God is offering.

When we display in our lives God's gift of this new life in Christ, others sense a real difference in us. They begin to realize that their own thirst is for God, their creator. They come to know their longing can be quenched. The invisible God becomes more visible through those who believe, as Christians share the *agape* love of God. But, it is by the power of the Holy Spirit who indwells believers that others come to know God. The Lord wants to display His glory so others can come to know their need for His living presence in their life.

> *Agape* love can be tangible when believers put
> action behind their words.
> Not only is love seen in their countenances, but in their deeds.
> God's love in them shines forth as a radiance of splendor.
> God is a fountain of living water that pours out to
> those who accept His gift of love.
> His presence can be felt when we need Him most.

Each spring, for a number of years, several churches in the Puget Sound area gathered for a three-day gospel festival. The

Christian bond was strong among them as believers lifted their voices in praise to God in the Bible college chapel. Each evening, there were many inspiring songs, and an evangelist or preacher would share a tremendous gospel message. I recall the music leader was a devoted lady with a powerful voice that caused others to rejoice in a splendid way in song. Those hymns were filled with fundamental Bible truths and praise that made them marvelous teaching tools of God's principles.

A sense of joy filled the air, and the presence of God was amazingly strong. One extremely gifted pianist performed marvelously as his fingers flew over the keys, and the beautiful tunes flowed outward and filled the chapel. A soloist or other musical groups contributed to the atmosphere, moving the crowd with their singing. Those events were days to remember, for they were uplifting, reverent times of true worship.

Something special occurred each festival as God's people shared their joy in song and heard the Word of God preached faithfully. There was a radiance among the people gathered. As they left to return home, a sense of glory seemed to cover them. God's people were radiant and rejuvenated from the experience. His glory was visible in inner change that happened in the men and women present, because they had been renewed by His presence.

Those inspirational festival times helped hone my spiritual life and strengthen my belief in God and Christ, His Son. They were a unique part of my spiritual growth, and gave me a strong foundation for the latter years of my life. The sessions embedded truth in my inner being, so as a counselor helping clients, God's standard was second nature to me. I could use the principles to guide and direct their courses in life.

Review:

Something is different about God's people who truly have the living Spirit of God indwelling them. Out of love, God sends the power we need to live a profitable life. Others can visibly see the joy and contentment, happiness and peace in the believer's life.

Closing Remarks:

Agape love is seen in the deeds of believers.
True love isn't stagnant; it's living, moving, flowing continuously.
The rejuvenated life shows a radiance of which others are aware.
The inner man is renewed with inner strength coming from God.

Chapter Twenty-Eight

OUR CALLING

God gave to each of us our own gifts, talents, and abilities. Our personal areas of interest are the best place to start to find these, and to fulfill His plan for our lives. God's heavenly calling to life in Christ should result in our finding joyful ways to serve Him. We need to strive to be worthy of our calling in line with His desire and His will.

> Who has saved us, and called us with a holy calling, not according to our works, but according to His own purpose and grace which was granted us in Christ Jesus from all eternity.
> (2 Timothy 1:9)

Q: Have you discovered your place in God's kingdom?

A: Just before Jesus went to the cross, He showed the disciples one last act of service by washing their feet. He had come to serve in our redemption as God's great Savior. His apostles had walked with this humble servant everywhere, during His time of ministry on earth. They saw the Lord's compassionate touch work miraculous healings and do other powerful signs. With no regard for Himself in those last moments, Jesus' thoughts were still on serving and training others. One of His closing acts of service left on the disciples a lasting impression of what real humility is as He knelt and washed their feet.

This custom of washing the feet of weary travelers as they entered the homes of relatives or friends was a long established act of hospitality in eastern cultures. Most that traveled by foot felt especially welcomed by the extension of such an act of kindness, along with being given food and a place to rest.

As Jesus knelt that night before each disciple, something marvelous must have happened in the hearts of those men. They began to understand what Jesus was teaching by His example. The Lord washed the feet of men who had just been contending for a chief position in His kingdom. Jesus then said, "For I gave you an example that you also should do as I did to you" (John 13:15). He was emphasizing that just hearing His instructions was not enough, but carrying out His word in service was the main point. True love is reflected in such simple acts of kindness.

The Lord further said, "If you know these things, you are blessed if you do them" (John 13:17). Knowledge needs to be connected with action. Real greatness in the eyes of God comes to those who are willing to offer help to the needy around them. Jesus came to serve us by fulfilling our greatest need of forgiveness of our sins and restoration, but He also illustrated the way to a holy life.

The Lord Jesus wanted His followers to understand that to be loyal to Him they needed to become servants, meeting the needs of others. After Jesus' resurrection and ascension, these faithful followers, as His servants, spread the good news of the gospel. By doing so, His disciples followed His example. They felt the call to serve so strongly that they all gave their lives that others might know Jesus, the Son of God.

By demonstrating the truth in the way we live as Christians, our love toward others reflects that we who willingly serve Him, as Jesus demonstrated, have learned to be bond-servants of God. Using our talents and gifts in the way He has called us to gives us a real freedom to be all we were intended to be.

God operates from a totally different standard than the world around us. As our Creator, He is the sovereign ruler of our life. But He is a caring ruler who knows what is best for us. By recognizing our rightful place in His kingdom as His servants, we also acknowledge the immeasurable extent of our debt to God. We have been purified by Christ's death on the cross and given the privilege of entering into a personal relationship with His Father. This relationship will be extended beyond here and now, for our redemption is intended for all eternity. Both as our Creator and Savior, Christ desires our willing service and our personal fulfillment, which comes as we answer His holy calling on our life. Discovering God's purpose for us, as individuals, brings out our best, which helps us know ourselves better and what we can accomplish with our lives. We have real freedom in Christ!

The apostle John was given a glimpse into heaven and recorded that in the New Jerusalem, "the throne of God and of the Lamb shall be in it, and His bond-servants will serve Him" (Revelation 22:3). God is our Creator and Savior, who gives us a gift of an unquestionable place in His kingdom. Jesus Himself promised to prepare this place for us—a sanctified place of equality to belong and serve. We now have an opportunity to worship God by our service here and further our preparation for the eons to come in eternity.

Finding our calling moves us into a closer relationship with the Almighty One, who loves us most, who knows us best, who established our potential, and who desires only good for us. Responding to the One who seeks to guide and direct our lives, and who desires a lasting relationship with us, gives us a place in His kingdom. Serving such a Lord does not hinder who we are, but enhances every fabric of our being. The sooner we find our place means the less time we waste in developing all that we can possible be as His children. God knows us as individuals and calls us to serve where we truly belong. He blesses our lives as we serve Him and those around us. A calling means serving, but the result is a joyful heart, contentment beyond words, and a real sense of purpose in life. We will be finding what God intended us to become in eternity, while enjoying life to the fullest here by answering His call.

Serving here helps us prepare for eternal life in heaven with God.
Discovering early on who we are and what we can do
helps develop our gifts and talents to the fullest.
Being a servant is a high honor.
All we do for others is, in fact, a service to the Lord.
Performing services for God brings out the best in us.
There is no self-centeredness or selfishness in a true servant.

A lot of people who I saw as a counselor had not discovered their potential, nor really established areas in which they could serve. Thus, they were unhappy people, who did not know how to handle life's conflicts. In reality, most had sought to solve their problems in their own strength. This is something none of us can do successfully.

Learning to lean on God ties in with finding our talents and gifts, and then using them as members of His kingdom. This means we need to know who we are and what we can do best, as well as have a working relationship with God.

As a wife and mother, I was using part of my talents and abilities before God pointed out I should counsel others who were suffering in some way. But, I wasn't using all my gifts for the Lord, because I wasn't fully aware of them. Being a wife and mother developed my love for others, my patience in tight spots, and much self-discipline in handling unexpected events. Those also were talents that were necessary when working with discouraged and hurting people. Before the Lord added to my assignment as a homemaker and gave me the task of counseling others, God patiently allowed me to grow in those areas and strengthened others, as I learned how to nurture my own family.

Our real calling in life may not come as soon as we graduate from high school or even college. That inner urging toward some profession or life change may only come when we are mature enough to recognize it. God often moves us a step at a time toward our real work and service. The Lord called men from their profession as fishermen to be "fishers of men." Then Jesus worked with them personally for three more years before He sent them out to do their real work. God uses the extra time to make sure we are willing and ready to serve where He wants us to be. His calling may be demanding, but it is the most fulfilling of all work.

As my work as a counselor increased, I sensed a feeling of joy and real pleasure when a session went well and was successful. Moving others on toward learning how to handle life's conflicts brought a deep feeling of personal satisfaction to me. I knew my place in God's kingdom and it added a new measure of fulfillment in life.

Review:

We all have a calling. Finding our position in life and using all our talents for God results in our becoming all He intended us to be. Being a servant elevates us high in God's eyes. The more we give, the more satisfied we will be.

Closing Remarks:

God loves a cheerful giver and doer.
He desires that we live fulfilled lives.
His holy calling opens the way for us to find His plan for our life.
As we live for Him, we are worshipping the Creator—our God.

Chapter Twenty-Nine

THE BEST DEFENSE

Having God in our corner in a conflict is a guarantee, that no matter what battle we face, we will come out as conquerors. Our Commander-in-Chief has the resources to defend His people. Christians are in a spiritual battle against invisible forces. Despite the source of our problems, God's methods are sure. God can equip His own people to fight the battle, as long as we invite the Lord into all our circumstances.

> Thus says the Lord to you, "Do not fear or be dismayed
> because of this great multitude, for the battle
> is not yours but God's."
> (2 Chronicles 20:15)

Q: What is the best defense in every circumstance?

A: The winter months bring storms, destruction, inconveniences, delays, changes, accidents, and even death in some cases. In any event, everyday pleasures can turn to demands and to hardships in an instant. Such things as mudslides, floods, pass closures, avalanches, washed-out roads and sinkholes, electrical poles down, lack of transportation, accidents, pain, and suffering all cause overwhelming situations in our lives. In a moment, times of prosperity can become times of adversity.

In the Old Testament, Job had to face such times, and his factual comment remains with us today. This patriarch said, "The Lord gave and the Lord has taken away. Blessed be the name of the Lord" (Job 1:21b). Through all his personal troubles, Job "did not sin nor did he blame God" (v. 22). Job's reaction speaks volumes today to the Christian, for his confidence in God remained despite all his suffering—he accepted the circumstances without blaming God. He was completely resigned to the agonizing news of his losses, which included all his children. Faith in God was Job's support beam, even though he did not understand all that had happened, nor why.

King David, as a young man, was called on to face Goliath, the Philistine giant, who challenged Israel, the army of God. With just a slingshot and some stones, David went into hand-to-hand combat. But David's real success hinged on his faith in God to see him through the battle (1 Samuel 17:37), for David trusted God to deliver him.

Such difficult times in life aimed at a person or his personal property comes to all of us. Some are hit more severely than others, but in various ways we all are hurt by life. To the Christian, these hard moments are as useful as the good times, because that is when the grace of God falls on those who believe and ask for help. We can grow spiritually by the problems we endure. It is also God's way of clearing out the cumbersome things in our lives and getting us, as Christians, to remain focused on Him. In a cluttered and complicated world, the need to simplify becomes necessary at times, so we will remain devoted to Christ (2 Corinthians 11:3).

Sometimes the "storms" of life seem impossible and even unbelievable to overcome, but victory is possible when one possesses child-like faith in Almighty God, as both Job and David did. Conquering the storms, overcoming the hardships, and rising again to walk in faith through life are possible when we trust God completely. When attempting to handle life's devastating moments we must:

- Reject the discouraging words of others;
- Overcome our own doubts;
- Lay aside our feelings, which get in the way of ministering to others, and concentrate on what God can do;
- Don't allow the situation to shut down progress, but instead believe the event is useful and will have an end;
- Recognize the true nature of any battle in life one is called to face, for in every circumstance the issue is always spiritual;
- Remember that God does not expect a person to manage life alone;
- Realize success becomes a matter of faith in the living God to handle our needs.

It is faith that conquers, no matter what situation we face, or conflict we are called to endure. Christians are called to "walk by faith, not by sight" (2 Corinthians 5:7), for a man's own efforts are not enough. That is why it is necessary to place our unwavering trust in God! Picturing what life would be like if we do so may be difficult, but remember God often has a different purpose in mind for our lives than we can foresee. Faith is our real avenue of communion with God, since we are trusting in an invisible, spiritual being. Our circumstances, trials, and disappointments should result in a deeper and more meaningful relationship with God when we exercise faith as our defense. Each time we do, God's faithfulness proves to be true!

> Do not forget that God is Lord
> and defender of His own people.
> Turning to God acknowledges our need of help
> beyond our own abilities.
> In conflict we become strong by His might.
> We are to stand in faith, ready, prepared, protected,
> for the battle is God's.

As a counselor, I once was called by a distraught husband to come and help him with his out-of-control wife. She had kept him up most of the night screaming and hollering and making no sense. As soon as I stepped through their front door, the woman dashed around the couch into the entrance hallway screaming she would kill me. Those tense demonic situations can only be confronted by the power of God. As I inwardly prayed for God's protection, He immediately dropped her physically to the floor.

An invisible barrier had been placed between her and me that broke her attack, knocking her down. Within a few minutes, she came to and was her old self, pleasant and friendly. Surprisingly, I had seen no angel, but I have every reason to believe that one or more was present to meet my needs for protection.

More than once, God's angels have restrained someone from doing me bodily harm. Upset clients have vented their anger toward life and their situation by lashing out at me. Yet, by the power of the Holy Spirit, who guides my thoughts and words, there has been a restraining force working and keeping others from their desire to hurt me. The most recent event occurred when a burglar tried to enter my home in the middle of the night. He left plenty evidence that he had attempted to break in. I can only surmise how he was stopped from gaining entrance though, since he was not caught.

God's guarding angels patrol the earth to protect His children (Psalms 34:7, 91:11). We are told these spiritual beings are there to minister to God's people (Hebrews 1:14). In answer to our prayers (Daniel 9:21), they are sent by God to bring messages and to protect His people from physical harm, and act in our defense and minister to our needs. As fellow servants, they deliver God's messages, protect God's people, patrol God's earth, carry out God's punishment, worship God, and fight the evil forces instigated by the devil and his fallen angels.

Angels are created beings just as we are, but with supernatural powers, who are sent to carry out God's will in matters. Sometimes they take on human form and make their presence known directly. Other times, I have no doubt they simply carry out their tasks invisibly without our direct knowledge of their presence. Our best defense in any situation is to remain under the shadow of God's wings, for His watchful care brings about lasting protection for His people.

Review:

Many situations arise that call for extra protection in our world. God will aid us, if we remember to pray. In spiritual battles, we are more than conquerors when we turn to God. He is in control.

Closing Remarks:

Faith in God is our best defense.

Storms may seem impossible to come through, but nothing is impossible with God.

Walking by faith brings surprising results.

Our defense is secure under God's protective wings.

Chapter Thirty

THE NEW YEAR

We all look forward to something new: a new home, new clothes, new job, new vehicle, new vacation, and a new year. We have our hopes and dreams, and with great determination we strive to fulfill them. We pledge mentally, and even verbally, to do something special or different. But the best of resolutions aren't always easy to fulfill. Our expectations are sometimes greater than our ability to perform.

> That which has been is that which will be,
> And that which has been done is that which will be done.
> So there is nothing new under the sun.
> (Ecclesiastes 1:9)

Q: What can each New Year hold for Christian believers?

A. Each New Year offers a new beginning in our daily walk with the Lord. If we do our part in faithfully following Him, God blesses our lives. A partial list of what God offers includes the following ten items:

1. Peace, in the place of anxiety, when we remember to pray (Philippians 4:6-7).
2. Sleep for those who trust in God and express thanks to Him for rest (Psalms 3:5, 4:8).
3. An overflowing blessing for tithing when one faithfully returns a portion of what has been entrusted into his or her care (Malachi 4:8-11).
4. Sufficient mercy and grace to carry the believer through times of conflict and need (Hebrews 4: 15-16).
5. Sunshine and rain sent on all mankind, for God shows His love and mercy even on those who least deserve it, as well as blessing those who are obedient (Matthew 5:45).
6. Wisdom for daily events comes from God, who generously gives guidance to those who ask, for He desires that His followers lack nothing (James 1:4-5).
7. *Agape* love (the kind of love found only in Christ Jesus) is a match for any tribulation, distress, persecution, or need (Romans 8:35-39).
8. Victory over the schemes of the devil and death comes to those who are steadfast and faithfully involved in the work of the Lord (Ephesians 6:10-18; 1 Corinthians 15:57-58).
9. The Holy Spirit's divine power and gifts within His followers, who provides "everything pertaining to life and godliness," as Christians trust Him (Acts 1:8; 2 Peter 1:3).
10. The awesome reality of God's presence, for the indwelling nearness of the Lord Jesus works in our lives through the Holy Spirit, when we acknowledge Him (John 14:16-23; Matthew 28:20).

In the epistle of James, we read that every good thing and every perfect gift is from God, for He loves to bless the person who perseveres during life's trials (James 1:17). While there is much more offered by God to those who believe, the above-listed blessings lay a solid foundation for handling any new year. May we wisely evaluate the mentioned list, and begin applying each one to our own lives. When it is time to give an account to Him, the Lord will greet those who do this with "well done good and faithful servant" (Matthew 25:21). Christians have nothing to fear in any new year, nor can trying times discourage those who believe, for the Lord offers what is necessary to overcome our troubles and enjoy life.

The resolutions we often make are usually let fall by the wayside. We feel it takes too much energy, time, or ability to fulfill them, and we tend to slide back into our old ways shortly after the new year has started. The Lord warns that what we pledge to do is a vow before Him, and we should not make a promise unless we plan on carrying it out by fulfilling our word. We need to remain sincere about what we utter that we will do or not do, for it is better to not give our word than to break our vows (Ecclesiastes 5:4-5).

Each new day is an important time to rethink our
purpose and direction in life.
Adjust what needs to be changed.
Serving God is more important than all other options,
for dedicated service brings fulfillment and inner peace.
What may be new to us has already been tried by others.
Enjoy life by daily doing your best.

Review:

Our word should be as good as gold. People trust what we say, and breaking our word breaks relationships. We honor God by keeping our word, and we also glorify Him by being dependable. Making resolutions based on God's Word and keeping them gives us a solid foundation that will remain sure.

Closing Remarks:

As followers of Christ, our word should be reliable.

Thinking through our promises and resolutions first helps us see if we are capable of keeping them.

Being adventurous and open to challenges is good.

But, considering our schedules, abilities, desires, and interests should govern our future commitments.

Our pledges need our dedication. Each new year is a grand opportunity to honor God by living out our commitments.

Chapter Thirty-One

TIME FOR REVIEW

Not only a yearly review, but a daily review of our life is necessary! Always being prepared to be called home to God or for Christ's second coming is critical. To stand in His holy presence with confidence and joy, not in shame or regret, should be our motivating force, especially as believers. Death will come to all human beings until His return, and preparation is necessary to ensure the Lord will welcome us. Keeping our life holy should be our aim.

> For we must all appear before the judgment seat of Christ,
> so that each one may be recompensed for his deeds
> in the body, according to what he has done,
> whether good or bad.
> (2 Corinthians 5:10)

Q: Are you prepared for your life to pass in review before Christ, our Maker?

A: When each New Year rolls around, many consider their New Year's resolutions. Goals are commendable, but being prepared for the second coming of Christ should be our ultimate goal for each day of our life. It's critical!

The apostle Paul told the brethren at Rome that each Christian must "give an account of himself to God" (Romans 14:12). Also in the book of Ecclesiastes, the Holy Spirit inspired the author, Solomon the preacher, to write "fear God and keep His commandments . . . for God will bring every act to judgment" (Ecclesiastes 12:13-14). More than once, the Lord Jesus gave instructions for His followers to be ready for His second coming, for at that time judgment will come on all (Matthew 24:42-51). The Lord Himself, said, "Therefore everyone who confesses Me before men, I will also confess him before My Father who is in heaven" (Matthew 10:32).

Accepting Christ as our Lord and Savior is the first step. Living faithfully for Him is the next step. The author of Hebrews further declared that as Christians, we should also "fix our eyes on Jesus" (Hebrews 12:2). In keeping our focus on the Lord, we can remain determined to do His will. If we do these things, then we will be prepared for a warm welcome into the Lord Jesus' presence when He comes.

With each new year, we should rejoice greatly at all the possibilities open to us to serve the Lord. For before us lies 365 days of opportunity for fellowship with Christ Jesus and God, our Father. We should not need disasters before we exercise our faith in Almighty God. Instead, by our daily living we should serve Christ and extend love to God with all our heart, soul, mind, and strength (Mark 12:30). When we complete each task Christ gives us, then His perfect peace, contentment, and satisfaction will settle over our hearts and lives. By faithfully serving the Lord, we are living out His desire for our life and preparing to be in His presence for all eternity. Slowly, ever so slowly, that bond of closeness that comes from His presence will engulf our lives and carry with it no fear of facing His final review.

Because we have been washed in His blood, the Christian's outlook on life becomes different from a non-believer's view and outlook on things. Our purpose in life takes on new meaning. Our words, actions, and motives seek to remain in accordance with the will of God. Thus, being prepared for the second coming of Christ Jesus involves:

- Being washed in His blood by baptism into Christ Jesus (Romans 6:3);
- Setting our mind on God's Word to know His will and spiritual truths (Romans 8:5-6);
- Looking for God's plan and good in every situation (Romans 8:28);
- Concentrating on the pure things in life, not on worldly things (Philippians 4:8);
- Being determined to stay on the highway of holiness (Isaiah 35:8);
- Craving for Christ's righteousness in our life and remaining right with God (Matthew 6:33);
- Longing to be a peacemaker, merciful and gentle in nature (Matthew 5:9);
- Walking according to the Spirit and being led by Him throughout life (Romans 8:4);
- Seeking fellowship and intimate communion with our glorious Lord and other believers (1 Corinthians 1:9);
- Desiring and striving to please God in all things (Hebrews 11:5-6);

- Hungering to worship and obey our Creator daily and attending church fellowship (John 4:23-24);
- Exercising true repentance when we do fail and sin (1 John 1:9);
- Resting in the Lord by trusting Him (Psalm 37:7);
- Loving the Lord with all our heart, soul, mind, and strength, and loving others as ourselves (Mark 12:30-31);
- Always placing our hope in Him and clinging to Him (Romans 5:1-5).

As we strive to please God, new hope, everlasting happiness, peace of mind and strength will come from our relationship with Jesus, our Lord. We can enter each new year knowing we, as Christians, can have victory in our present life and the one to come.

> There are so many reasons for us to be grateful to God.
> Words cannot convey what Jesus suffered in our place.
> For our sins, He was separated from God for a span of time.
> On the cross, physical suffering, mental anguish,
> and spiritual separation
> were all laid on Him for the evil in our lives.
> We deserved God's punishment!
> Yet, Christ's humility, suffering, and mercy saved us.
> Don't ever underestimate what He has done.

When the boss calls us in for an evaluation of our work, we tend to have fear and dread as our companions. Unsure of what the results will be or even if we will remain on the job, we don't look forward to such an event. Any boss we might stand before in this lifetime will be looking at our mistakes, errors, and limitations. He will consider the quality and quantity of work we have done, and he will be comparing all that to his own goals and desires for his business.

But God's scales of judgment are different in that they weigh our abilities, our use of time, our opportunities, and our unselfish service done in obedience to His will. God weighs all aspects of the situation fairly, and He does this all with great love. His judgment is fair and right.

Our heavenly review before Christ will bring forth events and happenings that we have long ago forgotten. But God doesn't forget the good we have done. He only forgets the sins He has forgiven, after we have repented. Jesus will be a just judge, for He bases this assignment on God's will and His absolute truth (John 5:30).

Standing before our holy God will remind us of just how fortunate we are to be covered by Christ's righteousness. We are allowed to be in God's presence because of His grace. Nothing we have done will have gotten us into His presence. Humbly that day, we will bow before the King of kings and Lord of lords, as He reviews our life's story in heaven. That heavenly review will proclaim what our rewards will be for faithfully serving Him. Still, as God's children, we will have a place in His kingdom, even though the review may find some of our work lacking in blessing from God. As Christians, we should be looking forward to Christ's second coming and our future life with Him.

A daily review of our life is hard to do, for we tend to feel we lack time for such evaluation. But spending time scanning over our performance of the day may save us from a time of embarrassment before God later on. He is willing to forgive us when we ask. Our own review here and now might cause us to see a need for change.

Review:

Being prepared daily for Christ's coming is essential, for His appearance can happen at any time. Out of His love, the Lord warns us to be prepared. So a daily review of our life is better than a yearly review that soon fades away.

Closing Remarks:

We all will appear before the judgment seat of Christ. Believers will be rewarded for their life accomplishments. To stand in His holy presence, we must strive to be holy. Victory is possible by His grace.

Chapter Thirty-Two

WORTHY OF PRAISE

Mankind was created to worship its Creator. The thirsty soul that remains unsatisfied is one within a human being who fails to worship the Lord God Almighty. That inner craving that won't go away will remain unfulfilled until one's relationship has been restored with his or her Maker. Our Lord and our Savior deserves our praise, our honor, and our worship. He alone can quench that inner spiritual longing.

> Worthy art thou, our Lord and our God,
> to receive the glory and the honor and the power: for thou didst create all things, and because of thy will they were, and were created.
> (Revelation 4:11 ASV)

> Great is the Lord, and highly to be praised,
> And His greatness is unsearchable.
> (Psalm 145:3)

Q: Why should we lift our hearts in exaltation of the Lord God Almighty who is worthy of our praise?

A: As an act of devotion to our Creator, we should lift our voices in admiration to God for who He is, and for all His glorious acts of blessings to us. He has extended life, favors, guidance, promises, and benefits to His people. Out of love and devotion to our Maker, we need to review what we have to be thankful for and with our praise honor God, *who is the Creator of all things,* including all of us humans (Colossians 1:16-17).

The following list expresses some reasons why there should be a song of praise to God in our hearts:

- God has given us *light* in His Word that we may see the way to real life—out of spiritual darkness into the light of truth from God (Ephesians 1:8).
- He extends *faith* to us so we may believe and trust Him—unquestioning belief in God (Ephesians 2:8).
- He has offered *salvation* that we may be free from the bondage of sin—rescued from sin's penalty by God's grace (Matthew 1:21).
- The Lord grants *grace* that we may claim this free gift of eternal life—unlimited and unmerited favor from God (Hebrews 4:16).
- He proclaims the everlasting *truth* in His Word, so we may know His absolutes and walk in the path of decency and life, as a result of Christ's death on the cross (Proverbs 3:5-6).
- He pours out indescribable *peace* to those who draw near to Him all the time—harmony and serenity extended by God (Philippians 4:6).
- The Lord offers *hope* during our lifetime for our future good and a place with Him for all eternity—eternal life in God's presence (1 Peter 1:3).

- He becomes our rock of *strength* when we choose Him as our foundation in life—firm stability and support, a refuge under His wings (Matthew 7:24, 16:18).
- He is our *Good Shepherd* who tends, gathers, leads, and carries His flock. Out of love and commitment He laid down His life and rose to care for us (Isaiah 40:11; John 10:11).
- He has given the *Comforter* to help those who believe and obey Him. We are not alone—the Helper indwells believers (John 14:16, 26).
- He provides *sunshine and rain* so crops will prosper and we can be fed—God provides (Matthew 5:45).
- He extends to us all our *basic needs* when we first seek His kingdom and His righteousness (Matthew 6:31-33). We are lacking in nothing physically and spiritually (James 1:4).
- God becomes a *Father* to the fatherless and an Advocate for the widows, as well as to all who believe. Jesus pleads our cause before God (Psalm 68: 5).
- He *delivers* those who trust Him from the "snare of the trapper," the devil. God protects His own (Psalm 91:3; 2 Timothy 2:26).
- And God pours out overflowing *blessings* to those who give offerings and gifts back to Him. God showers His divine favor on believers (Malachi 3:10).
- All around us, His *wonders* are to be seen in nature, which inspire and lift our souls. Nature reveals the Creator (Romans 1:20).
- His *love* is extended to those who respond to the Creator's call to come to Him. Divine love is given (Revelation 22:12).

- He even *disciplines* those He loves to promote "our good that we may share His holiness"—training that nourishes self-control and character by the Holy Spirit (Hebrews 12:10).
- The Lord God *rescues* from death the souls of those who believe. Death is conquered by Christ's sacrifice (1 Corinthians 15:54).
- He becomes our *shield* of protection when the enemy hurls fiery darts. The Father guards and defends (Ephesians 6:11).
- God *carries* the load when we are weary. "Daily He bears our burden" (Psalm 68:19).
- He is our *hiding place* in times of trouble and moments when we need rest. The Lord covers and conceals His own (Psalm 32:7; Matthew 11:28).
- We are *redeemed* by the righteousness of Christ Jesus—freely given to those who believe (John 3:16, Romans 3:24-25).
- We are *cleansed* by Christ's blood from all of our sins—washed and made whiter than snow (1 John 1:7).
- Jesus, as our *High Priest* and *Mediator*, intercedes on our behalf, reconciling us to God, His Father and our God, and offers our prayers to the Almighty on our behalf (1 Timothy 2:5).

Do not fear, nor become anxious when life becomes rough. God will remove weariness and will infuse new strength into those who trust in the Lord. "The name of the Lord is a strong tower; the righteous runs into it and is *safe*" (Proverbs 18:10, emphasis added).

God is gracious, merciful, and sustains His people. He gives new life, new vigor, new significance, and godly qualities to those who acknowledge Him. "Praise the Lord! How blessed is the man who fears the Lord" (Psalm 112:1). That kind of fear means deep reverence, not dread or apprehension.

Because God is who He is, our Creator and Lord, and for all He has done to reconnect mankind back to Himself, our praises of gratitude should flow freely from genuine, overwhelmed hearts. But, our praises should include appreciation for what God daily does for us too. His commitment to us is for our whole lifetime and all of eternity, not just that we might be saved from sin. God's love is permanent and everlasting.

> As created beings, praising God should be our top objective.
> Honoring our Sustainer and Giver of life—God Himself—
> should come from a truly grateful heart.
> By entrusting ourselves to His care, we are kept safe.
> Out of deep devotion to our Lord and Protector,
> loving praise from the heart should automatically emerge.
> Our God is the God of the past, the present, and the future
> and should be adored and honored.

Review:

That inner longing we each share can only be quenched by a relationship with God. Nothing else we may try will work. Satisfaction and inner peace comes when our broken relationship is reestablished with our Maker. Mankind has within a deep desire to worship, but often tries to fill this need by other means. Songs of praise and our prayers of gratitude should express our admiration for Almighty God, as they flow from our lips.

Closing Remarks:

Instead of giving our adoration to worldly things, our feelings of devotion and love should go directly to God.
Nothing should come between Him and us.
We have many reasons to respect the Creator and worship Him.
God made us to have a relationship with Him.

Who is worthy to be praised?

Christ Jesus was despised and rejected by His own people.
The truth He brought was held in disbelief.
A man of compassion, He ministered to the downtrodden.
Anointed by God as the Messiah—the Deliverer—
He was sent to proclaim release to the captives.
The Lamb of God was lead to slaughter.
The Light of the world was put out in our place.
He bore the punishment all deserved.
The Man of Sorrow was acquainted with grief.
The way to God was opened by His death, burial, and resurrection.
The life He bought was meant for all who believe.
The man of compassion, the divine Son of God,
has given His all on our behalf.
Now He waits to welcome His children home.
Jesus, the Son of God!
Praise His holy name!

Who is worthy to be praised?
The Lord God Almighty.

Other Titles by Georgia Gorham-Brockman:

The Counselor's Corner: Reveals a Better Way
Above and Beyond: Heaven-Homeward Bound
He Stays With Me: The Realness of God
Quest for the Abundant Life: The Depth of the Master Artist's Love
The Master Communicator: Life-Changing Questions Jesus Asked

Contact Information

To order additional copies of this book, please visit
www.redemption-press.com.
Also available on Amazon.com and BarnesandNoble.com
Or by calling toll free 1-844-2REDEEM.

CPSIA information can be obtained
at www.ICGtesting.com
Printed in the USA
FSOW02n0057160415
6384FS

9 781632 322524